# "Ah, LIFE"

## Another Brick in the Wall

A Self-Development Guide including
positive Hypnotic Suggestions

By Helen Skene

Illustrations by John Gordon

### LIFE

(Cambridge Dictionary definition)

The period between birth and death, or the experience or state of
being alive

### ANOTHER BRICK IN THE WALL

(Pink Floyd's metaphor)

An event that has caused you to become more alienated and distant
with something such as society or a relationship

With special thanks to

Kayleigh, Becky, Richard, Jeremy, Christine, John and Colin for their support, encouragement, expertise, talents and editing.

And, of course, to my mum and dad.

# CONTENTS

# INTRODUCTION

The fact that you are reading this leads me to believe you are not feeling entirely content. Maybe you have a home, a job, a relationship and maybe a great family, and yet you do not feel okay. Externally your life is okay and internally it is not. Perhaps it is not okay externally either.

I'm guessing you would like to make changes to yourself or your life and that you've tried various self-improvement ideas and, like a memory-foam pillow, you've reverted to form. No matter how much money, willpower or sheer determination you throw at making changes, your original behaviours return. You are not alone. This is normal human behaviour and does not mean that you are a failure, although it can feel that way at times.

I'd like to offer you an insight into why your best efforts are being sabotaged and how to overcome this; to explain why your subconscious secretly pulls you back to a familiar uncomfortable place when consciously you want to move forward; to help you discover how your parents changed you into their version of who you *should* be; how you adapted yourself to survive your environment, and by doing so created the Blueprint for the rest of your life.

(The use of the word **parents** in this guide incorporates birth parents, foster parents, adoptive parents and primary carers of infants. Although other carers, such as family members, school teachers, adults from religious bodies, friends and exposure to social media would have a significant impact on a child in later life, it is their earliest bonds that are most important in forming the Blueprint.)

Throughout this guide I have used the analogy of building a brick Tower, from the Groundwork, Foundation and Framework to the

Brickwork, Wiring and Windows, to describe the various stages of change and development which has transformed you from pre-birth to the person you are today with your pre-defined Blueprint.

According to Song Meanings and Facts' Jessica Shelton, in rock band Pink Floyd's Another Brick in the Wall track: "The narrator systematically reveals the major events in his life that cause him and many other people to detach themselves mentally from the outside world. That is to say, he literally uses those reasons as 'bricks' to build a wall. And this wall separates and at the same time protects him from being hurt by the rest of the world."

The metaphor 'another brick in the wall' has also been used to describe how people are conditioned to behave in expected ways in order to conform with society. Each person is represented by a brick, and the wall is symbolic of the society in which they live.

When people are moulded into a prerequisite state, usually by their parents, they can lose their individuality, special uniqueness and sense on self. They simply become 'another brick in the wall'.

Although most of your conditioning would have been with the conscious aim of keeping you safe and acceptable within society, some subconscious learned behaviours would have caused you to adapt in ways that may have helped you feel safe as a child but no longer serve you well as an adult.

This book is not about blaming parents or anyone else for the way you are; it is a fact finding mission to help you understand your predicament and enable you to move on from it. It encourages you to become aware of your own Blueprint and discover why you think, feel and behave the way you do and why these behaviours create the same repeating results in your life. It will help you find out what holds you back from making the changes you desire and support you to create a new Blueprint for the rest of your life.

At the end of each chapter is an exercise of ten questions encouraging you to think about who you are and why you think, feel and behave as you do. You can either reflect on the questions or write down your answers for future reference.

Before we discover who you are I'll introduce myself. I'm a mother, daughter, sister, psychotherapist, hypnotherapist, writer and Reiki teacher. All these labels go a long way to describing my interest in people and my desire to help by offering empathy, education and optimism.

For many years my life felt like a crazy roller coaster. I would achieve the life I wanted, it would turn sour and I'd desire something new. It was like I was constantly moving up and down and back and forth and never moving consistently forward. I blamed others for my frustrations.

Then I had four years of personal counselling and recognised that I was the common denominator in my turbulent life and it was my Blueprint that created the repeat cycles that caused my heartache. The great news was, that if I was the one repeating the cycles, I was also the one in control of changing them.

Around 35 years ago I was a receptionist with limited qualifications and a desire to become a newspaper journalist.

As I waited in the tension-heavy pre-interview room I regarded the other candidates in their smart suits. I listened as they discussed universities and media degrees. Each had a highbrow newspaper tucked under their arm. I had forgotten to polish my shoes.

I was faced by a daunting panel of five who questioned me at length about my qualifications (six GCSE equivalents and a hairdressing diploma). My choice of preferred newspapers? (The Sunday Mirror when dad bought it.) My choice of personal interest reading? (Danielle Steel romances borrowed from mum.)

Despite it all, editor David Henshall offered me a position as trainee journalist and his words stayed with me: "Some people are educated, articulate writers, but they can't connect with people in order to hear their stories. We can teach you how to write." A backhanded compliment, but one I was willing to accept.

I became a journalist and rubbed shoulders with the great and famous (an exaggeration). As if playing a real-life game of Snakes and Ladders I had rolled a six, shot to the top of the tallest ladder and left behind the familiar struggle at the end of the snake.

Despite having journeyed to the dizzy heights of my dream job, it was not many years before my subconscious covertly pulled me back to a familiar position. Sliding down that snake was in line with my Blueprint.

Self-doubt, criticism, humiliation and guilt all encroached from within me like a fungus spreading emotionally outward until my external world reflected my internal struggle. Again, I was back at the beginning of the game.

It was time to regroup and restart. This was a repeat cycle and it happened numerous more times before I made permanent changes to my Blueprint.

During my last years as a journalist I was a court reporter retelling how criminals had behaved and been punished. I heard mitigation of how their former lives had led to their behaviour and then often to their remorse. Reporting their stories never sat well with me but it did pay the bills and further cemented my interest in why people think, feel and behave as they do.

I then retrained as a psychotherapist and hypnotherapist which included mandatory personal counselling. Through this I became aware of how my childhood Foundation and Framework had helped to set a Blueprint for my life.

I was able to recognise the consequential impacts on any future life I tried to build. I was able to see the game of Snakes and Ladders from a different perspective and from that viewpoint I could play with awareness or choose not to play.

I must add here that my parents are wonderful, loving people who did their very best to ensure I had a comfortable childhood and grew into a socially acceptable person. Little did they know, or did I know when I became a parent, that there were so many hidden pitfalls.

It is often the case that low self-esteem can be continued through generations of families with parents raising children with low self-esteem and, when they grow up and have children of their own, the cycle repeats. This is all the more reason to grow healthy high self-esteem now. And that is precisely what this guide encourages you to do.

During my own Tower excavation, I discovered there were some questionable building materials in my Groundwork and Foundation that had caused my Tower of Life to crack and crumble. I learned how I used relationships and alcohol as Scaffolding to keep my Tower from falling, and I found out how growing self-esteem could Underpin my Tower and allow me to feel worthy of the abundance life has to offer.

I hope this down-to-earth therapy manual provides a practical and light-hearted insight into your own Blueprint and offers you the guidance to Underpin your Tower for a future life of contentment.

# YOU TODAY
# YOUR TOWER

Describing psychology by way of Snakes and Ladders and Towers may be unconventional, but the building of a Tower is a particularly useful analogy when understanding the growth and development of humans.

How you are today was mainly determined by how you as a child, were conditioned by your parents. Your parents and their behaviours were your Foundation and they created your Framework by using conditioning methods of praise and punishment. The rest of your life was built on and around this Foundation and Framework.

Maybe you have played the game of Jenga where three wooden blocks are placed at right angles on top of the three wooden blocks below them until a tower of blocks are built.

The players then take it in turn to carefully remove one block at a time from below the top layer while trying to avoid the tower crashing to the ground. If those first few layers of blocks (the Foundation) are not placed squarely against one another the rest of the tower becomes unstable.

In psychology, a secure person has a solid Foundation of love, support and guidance from assertive parents with healthy self-esteem. The Foundation of an insecure person would likely contain love, support and guidance, but interwoven with the fear of passive or aggressive parents with low self-esteem. Their Foundation is unstable.

It is important to acknowledge here that people are not only assertive, passive, aggressive or passive-aggressive; or simply have high or low self-esteem; or are just secure or insecure. Thoughts, emotions and behaviours span a wide spectrum and people can feel differently during different times of their lives, and in fact during different times of a day.

However, people do have a propensity to have lower self-esteem or higher self-esteem based on their Foundation. By developing healthier self-esteem they are more likely to feel better about themselves and more deserving of getting their needs met.

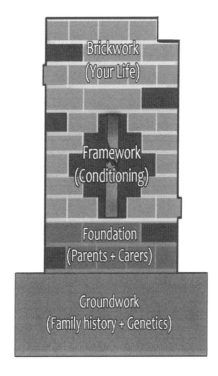

**Your Tower has Groundwork, Foundation, Framework and Brickwork**

Your family history and genetics formed the **Groundwork** on which your **Foundation** was laid.

Your **Foundation** represents your parents' values and behaviours, based on their family history.

Your **Framework** represents the mould your parents set you in by way of conditioning, based on their values.

Your **Brickwork** represents the life you've built around that **Framework**, using the **Blueprint** all the above created.

When there are questionable materials in your **Groundwork** and **Foundation**, the **Framework** becomes unstable and this is repeated in the **Brickwork** which causes your **Tower** to crack and crumble.

We'll look later at how your conditioning formed the **Wiring** that became your internal workings; the **Windows** that represent your perspective of yourself and the world in which you live; the **Scaffolding** which represents your ways of coping with inner turmoil, and how all these go to make up your **Blueprint** for life.

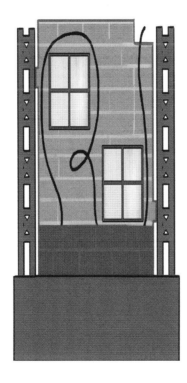

**Your Tower has Wiring, Windows and Scaffolding**

When you try to make changes to yourself it is also your conditioning and learned behaviours that produce **Snagging**, which is representative of your resistance to change. **Snagging** can include conscious and unconscious reasons to stay as you are, such as: "If I stop smoking I'll be grumpy" or "people will not like me if I change". Once you work through the **Snagging** list, **Underpinning** can be carried out. **Underpinning** represents the changes that you can achieve to alter your **Blueprint** permanently.

Where are you today? Maybe you are at work, at home or in a garden. This is the proximity of your physical self to your external world. Your external world is likely to have an affect on your internal feelings.

Equally, how you feel on the inside is likely to cause you to create the external world in which you live, such as subconsciously keeping yourself in a low paid job because you have low self-worth. By changing your internal world (or Blueprint), everything else changes too (the Ripple Effect).

Where you are and how you are today is like looking out from within your Tower. You hold certain beliefs about how the Tower should look and feel inside and out. You look through your Windows, and your perspective of your Tower and what lies beyond depends on the clarity and distortions of the glass.

Your Tower's Wiring and Windows were mainly created by your parents who conditioned you to think, feel and behave in certain ways.

**The Ripple Effect**

The sum of everything that has ever happened to you creates your thoughts, feelings and behaviours, and results in how your Tower is today. If you were to compress your Tower into one tiny rock and drop it into a pool of water you could watch the Ripple Effect you have on everything external to you: your family, your friends, your work etc. It is difficult to change the ripples (especially if they represent people), but by changing the Tower, the ripples change naturally as a side-effect.

Your Tower was built by you, using the Blueprint that your parents gave you, based on the Blueprint their parents gave them.

Please be under no illusion that anything external to you is creating your discomfort. Your discomfort comes from within you, from your Blueprint of your Tower, and only by achieving change there, will you manifest change throughout the ripples.

Put another way, imagine yourself stuck in a traffic jam. You are sitting in your car and not going anywhere fast. Are you the angry driver who is banging your steering wheel and shouting abuse at the other road users?

Are you the anxious driver scared witless that your boss might fire you for being late? Or are you the driver who switches on the radio and kicks backs their heels thinking: "Well, I can't go anywhere, so I might as well relax and enjoy being slowed down for a while"?

Notice that the actual traffic jam is the same for everyone. The traffic jam is external to all the drivers. The difference is their internal worlds. Their interpretation based on their Wiring and their perspectives from their Windows, has created the meaning they have individually placed on the event.

You may question here: "What about if I'm usually calm, but I'm in a hurry and the traffic jam has made me anxious and angry?"

Yes, the relaxed driver is capable of feeling angry or anxious if the traffic jam prevents him or her getting somewhere on time, but they are less likely to be consumed or overwhelmed by their feelings.

It is no coincidence that angry people regularly come across people who 'make them angry' and anxious people regularly find themselves in situations that 'make them anxious'.

No one and nothing can 'make you feel' anything. Your feelings come from within you. They belong to you. They are your responsibility.

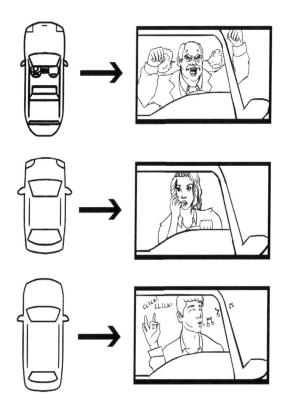

**The Traffic Jam**

When you begin to see how this all works it makes sense why it is important to focus on changing your internal rather than your external world. Of course, it is easier to protest that your external environment is preventing you  from changing than it is to take responsibility for yourself and face your fears.

14

**Fears**

Your fears are created by you (in your subconscious) when you *think* of what making the changes might mean.

Initially you may decide that you want to practise saying "no" to people in order to show them you have respect for yourself and in return receive more respect from them, in order to grow your self-esteem. Sounds simple enough doesn't it?

Your resistance (or Snagging) starts when you begin to **think** about actually doing something. You think of a scenario such as: "When my son next asks if I can lend him some money, I will simply say no." Then you think: "He won't be very happy about that. He might ignore me or stop me seeing his children or just not like me any more."

This line of thinking will cause you to **feel** anxious, rejected or helpless and your **behaviour** will be influenced by these feelings. Most likely you will do what you always do (your **habit**) and lend him some money, whilst telling yourself: "It's no big deal, I have enough," in order to justify your actions and feel better about your lack of assertiveness.

**Change**

Change is scary and it is scary because you have been conditioned to **fear** being anything other than what your parents wanted you to be. You learned, just as I did, that if you do as you are told you will feel okay and if you do not do what you are told you will not feel okay. You and me and they were conditioned to think, feel and behave in ways that conform to our family beliefs, values and rules, and those of society.

A child  not only conforms to how their parents want them to be, but they (and their parents) are also influenced by their wider environments. American psychologist Urie Bronfenbrenner formulated the Ecological Systems Theory to explain how children typically become enmeshed in various ecosystems, from their close family and school systems, to the most expansive systems of society and culture.

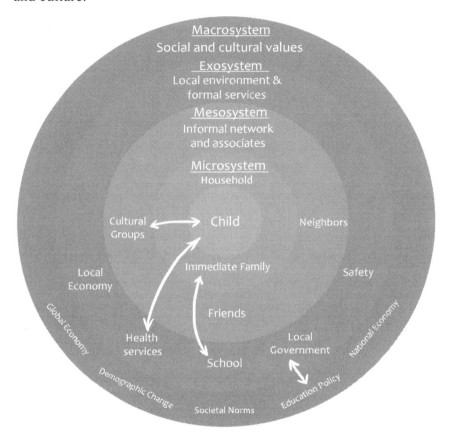

**Bronfenbrenner's Ecological Systems Theory**

These ecosystems (Micro, Meso, Exo and Macro systems) show the different levels at which a child is influenced. At the same time that this is impacting on a child, all the people who have contact with that child are also enmeshed in their own variations of these ecosystems.

Also, each of these people are influenced by their own family history (Groundwork); parents (Foundation) and conditioning (Framework), and like most human beings they wish to be accepted within their sphere of community and fear rejection from it.

The one thing most people want in this life is to be accepted, and what most people fear is rejection.

In the past it may have seemed easier to do what other people wanted you to do rather than to be assertive and say what you would prefer. You may have been afraid to 'rock the boat' or 'go against the grain' just in case someone thought less of you because they might feel some emotional discomfort and blame you. You needed to feel liked to avoid your fears of rejection.

Now you realise that you were allowing dominating people to take advantage of you and you were encouraging their behaviour. You now see that these dominating people were afraid of being rejected. They needed to feel in control to avoid their fears of rejection.

Just by reading this book so far, you may be aware of your inner voice trying to prevent you from reading on. Your conditioning will be strong and your subconscious has resisted change. Your brain is very clever and will try to trick you into staying as you are. Your inner voice may be telling you that you won't be any good at changing so there's no point in trying; it may be trying to guilt you into believing you should be doing something, anything else other than reading this book; it may be distracting you with thoughts of food or a drink to lure you away.

If you are experiencing any of these or other sabotaging thoughts, that is great, because you are becoming aware of your internal workings. If you keep with it you will notice that wonderful subconscious resistance (Snagging) that holds you back from becoming anything other than who you have always been.

## Habits

Your subconscious is designed to keep you alive (rather like an over-zealous bodyguard), so as long as you are alive it will continue to ensure you keep doing the same things you have always done, and it does this by creating habits.

I remember on the Trisha Show years ago, she said if you always use the same bait you'll always catch the same fish. That is so true. We are all creatures of habit and those habits have been bred into us since we were tiny babies and we've developed a few of our own along the way.

We have been conditioned, brainwashed, moulded, nurtured and bullied into becoming the people we are today.

You have developed habits and **beliefs** that you replay over and again through your inner dialogue with yourself to such an extent that you may have no idea where your views and opinions start and your parents' input ends.

As a child you may have been conditioned to believe you had to put others before yourself and to  put their needs above your own. You are not responsible for protecting other people's feelings, especially if it is to the detriment of your own feelings.

## Messages

Through the words, gestures, looks, tones of voice, actions and non-actions of your parents, you developed a sense of self and your value in the world. The childhood messages you received gave you unique filters (or Windows) based on that value.

It was a bit like being given a pair of glasses with a prescription that reflected your value. These glasses impact on the way you think. Your thoughts have a direct effect on your feelings; your feelings guide your behaviours and your behaviours get results. Your feelings are always valid, but the thoughts on which they are based are sometimes distorted, depending on the quality of your glasses.

All this has been going on for all the years you have lived, and in the main, you probably had no clue. It was not within your awareness. Now it is within your awareness and, because of this, subtle positive changes are already taking place within you.

When you have high self-esteem you respect yourself and see yourself differently. When you see yourself more favourably you feel better about yourself, other people and the world in which you live.

Healthy self-esteem develops when you behave assertively. When you live your life on purpose you are using assertive behaviour. You have  decided the way you wish to live your life and know you have every right to live it that way.

## Questions:

At the end of each chapter is a list of questions to encourage you to think more about yourself and to raise your awareness about why you think, feel and behave as you do today. It could be helpful to write your answers in a note book or journal along with any thoughts, feelings or memories that arise during these exercises.

## Who are you today?

1. How do you feel emotionally? (e.g. neutral, happy, content, sad, overwhelmed, peaceful)

2. How is your mental health? (e.g. anxious, depressed, paranoid, confused, over-thinking)

3. How is you physical health? (e.g. unwell, lethargic, painful, energised, aching, healthy)

4. How do you feel about yourself as a person? (e.g. kind, selfish, worthless, loveable)

5. How do you feel about yourself physically? (e.g. overweight, underweight, attractive, beautiful)

6. Do you put others before yourself? (e.g. giving to others to your own detriment)

7. Do you think others are out to get you? (e.g. distrustful or sceptical of people's motives)

8. Do you feel good enough? (e.g. thinking you *should* be better than you are to please others)

9. Do you have high expectations of yourself? (e.g. feel pressure to reach very high goals)

10. Rate your life 0 awful – 10 fantastic:

Romantic/sexual relationships

Family relationships

Friendships

Home environment

Leisure activities

Employment

Education

Finances

Coping methods (e.g. alcohol, over working, excessive cleaning etc)

# FAMILY HISTORY AND GENETICS
# YOUR GROUNDWORK

Let's go back to the very beginning. Do you think this would have been when you were conceived or when you were born? How about when your grandmother or your grandmother's grandmother, or your ….... yep keep going….. was conceived or born?

**The Domino Effect**

Your family history is like an extremely long line of standing dominoes. The first one was pushed and toppled, and as each domino fell against the next it affected the one that followed.

Thousands of years ago one of your ancient relatives was born and whoever gave birth to them passed on their genetics to that baby.

**The Domino Effect**

That ancient relative would have also created an environment for the baby; they would have their own methods of parenting (probably based on how they were parented), and their own issues based on their parents' genetics, environment, experiences, parenting skills and issues (meaning their Groundwork, Foundation and Framework).

The dominoes kept falling, one against the other, until eventually your mother was born and she inherited the genes of her parents; their style of parenting; the environment they lived in; and their behaviours, values and beliefs.

Around the same time your father was also being born with his unique set of behaviours, values and beliefs from his parents.

All these behaviours, values, beliefs, strengths, weaknesses, habits, fears, family rules, nutrition, disease, culture, social norms and faiths were passed on through the Domino Effect from generation to generation until one day you became an egg in your mother while she was still a foetus inside your grandmother. Mind-blowing!

This state of affairs becomes even more complex when children are brought up by carers other than their birth parents, who again, have their own set of behaviours, values and beliefs.

Long before you were born your Groundwork was already well established. Genetics, environments, cultures, society, world wars, family economics, illness, and many other influences, moulded your parents or primary carers, and created their own unique sets of behaviours, beliefs and feelings about themselves (their Wiring and Windows).

In other words, throughout the thousands of dominoes before you, every person in your family history had their own Towers with Groundwork, Foundation, Framework, Brickwork, Wiring and Windows, which sculptured their internal worlds and caused their views of their external worlds. With all this running through them, your parents then developed you.

You were a helpless, vulnerable baby who was totally dependent on these folk for your every need, nutrition, shelter and nurture. Your subconscious quickly recognised the value of these people for your survival and clung onto every movement they made and every word they said. Whatever they did, whatever they said, however they behaved, was going to inform you of who you were and what was expected of you.

The first 18 months of your life was also the most influential.

**The Metaphorical Mirror**

Metaphorically, your parents held up a mirror and showed you who you were by their  actions, gestures, facial expressions, tones of voice, silence or words. The subconscious behaviours and facial expressions of parents with low self-esteem will impact on a child's self-esteem as much, if not more than the words they use.

It is worth pointing out here that the majority of parents want what they think is best for the baby and they can only give that infant what they have available to them, emotionally and intellectually.

However, the way your parents were praised and punished in order to be conditioned as children, was probably the method they would have used to condition you. Also, you would have subconsciously watched their every behaviour and learned from them. This would mainly happen outside of your parents awareness and certainly outside of yours.

**Questions:**

As you think about these questions you may notice similarities between your grandparents, parents and yourself. It may also be useful to draw a simple family tree at this stage to give yourself a visual image of your place in your family and how traits have passed through generations.

**Who were your grandparents?**

1. What were your grandparents like physically at your age?

2. What were your grandparents like emotionally?

3. What were their lifestyles like?

4. What was their line of work?

5. How would you and your parents describe their personalities?

6. What was their relationship with each other like?

7. What were their hobbies?

8. What vices did they have?

9. How was their health when they were your age?

10. What were their characteristic mannerisms or favourite phrases?

# YOUR PARENTS
# YOUR FOUNDATION

Finding out who your parents were will help you go a long way to discovering who you are.

How would you describe your parents' behaviours when you were a child? Were they assertive, passive, aggressive or passive-aggressive? Were they rigid and straight or fun and spontaneous? What was their sense of humour like? Did they have a positive or negative attitude toward life? Did they use alcohol, work, drugs, exercise, gambling or other methods to feel better? Did they use any controlling methods, routines, restrictions, perfectionisms, or criticisms in order to feel okay? What did they do for work? Were they consistently loving and supportive, even when you did something wrong, or critical and disparaging? Did they look after and rescue people or animals? Did they get angry and judge others? Were they bossy and know it all? Did they behave as if they were incapable of looking after themselves? Were they kind and caring and know what was best for others? Did they appear vulnerable or almost childlike?

How often have you hoped you would or wouldn't become like your parents, and how often have people commented on how much you are like them?

**Beliefs**

I'm not saying you became a carbon copy of your parents, but how they viewed themselves and others would influence how you see yourself and others. There may be times when you, as a grown-up, with your knowledge through education and life experiences may not agree with your parents' behaviours, but some aspects of their behaviours may be familiar and compelling to you. This can manifest into thinking you dislike something they do, but actually you are in denial that it is true of you also.

Your parents' beliefs will stay with you on some level even when you don't want them to. For example, if your parents had a strong religious ethic and brought you up with these beliefs, and as an adult you decide you no longer wish to be religious, those beliefs will remain at your subconscious core regardless of whether you want them to influence you or not.

This is why sometimes you can experience logically knowing something for sure and yet irrationally believing the opposite (such as knowing you are reasonably intelligent, but believing your are feeble-minded; or, knowing you are slim, but believing you are over-weight).

I particularly notice this with clients suffering with lower self-worth. Logically they *know* they have worked hard to achieve their title of, let's say, headteacher and they know they are deserving of the benefits this title brings. However, at the same time they can *feel* undeserving of the title, as if they are a fraudster soon to be found out, and incapable of holding this position and undeserving of the salary. This 'imposter syndrome' is very common.

Perhaps the parents of this headteacher suffered with lower self-worth and their behaviours subconsciously told their offspring that this is who they were too.

**Rules**

Family rules can also be passed from generation to generation, to your parents and then to you. These are your family's own set of rules based on the family beliefs, similar to a religion or culture, but individual to your family. They may include behaviours and beliefs such as: it is normal to have roast dinner on Sunday; tall, slim people are desirable; people who do not work hard are lazy; we pretend bad things don't happen in this family; boastful people are not liked; children should be seen and not heard; mother does everything for everyone; you should pick yourself up and get on with it; the men in this family watch sport.

A family member who doesn't conform to the family standard is often negatively judged by the family.

You conformed to your family rules because a) they were normal to you and you learned by copying b) you were conditioned by means of praise and punishment (love and fear) to conform, and c) you developed habits and beliefs which ensured the behaviours were repeated.

Humans want to be accepted and fear being rejected. It's that simple and probably comes from the baby brain quickly learning how to get needs met in order to survive.

You spent much of your life subconsciously weighing up which behaviours would give you the most pleasure (being praised or feeling accepted) or avoid the most pain (being chastised or feeling rejected).

These learnings helped to cement your Framework in place so you think, feel and behave in certain ways in accordance with your parents' values.

This form of conditioning, or brainwashing, created your Smart Brain (Wiring and Windows) which effectively and efficiently operates you on a subconscious level so you don't even have to think about your actions. You simply react to stimuli on autopilot, rather than responding consciously.

When a child responds consciously they may be actively going against their parents' rules in order to get what they desire, or they may not realise they are not conforming due to confused beliefs.

As children we were conditioned with rules of how to behave and what to do and what not to do and this created submissive children who grew up to be passive adults. You no longer have to follow those rules because you are not a child any more and you can make your own rules.

Your Foundation will depend on your parents' Groundwork, Foundation and Framework. Your parents' Foundation and therefore your Foundation was laid on the Groundwork of your ancestors. Was yours a solid granite flat surface or a bumpy rubble and sand base?

When you look at your Foundation look at how your parents were when you were a child rather than how they are now. As a grown-up you may have a very different relationship with your parents because you are now all adults, and this may have changed the Ripple Effect (how your behaviour influences the behaviour of others). The way you are now was learned in your childhood from how you perceived your parents then.

If your Groundwork and Foundation were unstable you can bet your Tower is going to have a wobble to it.

**Questions:**

Think about what your answers mean to you and how your own thoughts, feelings and behaviours relate to your answers.

**Who were your parents?**

1. Were your parents mainly passive, aggressive, passive-aggressive or assertive?

2. How were your parents praised as children?

3. How were your parents punished as children?

4. Are your parents more responsible or irresponsible?

5. Did your parents have any strong beliefs?

6. How did your parents react if you were upset?

7. Describe your parents, each in three words?

8. What did your parents do for work?

9. What did your parents do for fun?

10. Were your parents positive or negative about life?

# CONDITIONING YOUR FRAMEWORK

Your parents formed your Foundation and used various conditioning methods by way of praise and punishment aiming to create the best version of you that they could. By the time you were a toddler your Framework was set on your Foundation. Your Framework mirrored the Foundation-base and grew up from it.

You subconsciously mimicked your parents' behaviours and continued to fit the mould they had set for you. Their methods of conditioning ensured you didn't veer off track too far, and the development of your Smart Brain (your internal Wiring and Window view) soaked up all this information and internalised it.

This efficient system made it easier for you to follow the rules automatically without having to think about them.

The automatic nature of acting without thinking is also why changing these behaviours is a challenge.

The Metaphorical Mirror told you who you were; you learned your parents' behaviours without even realising it; through following the pain and pleasure principle you were moulded into believing their beliefs and behaving how they behaved or wanted you to; and you developed a sense of self and your value in comparison to others.

As well as your parents consciously conditioning you with praise and punishment, you would also have been conditioned subconsciously by watching and copying their behaviours, gestures, mannerisms, preferences and by reading their facial features.

By the time you became adolescent (and probably earlier) you had a full set of beliefs of who you were; your sense of self-worth; what was expected of you; what you were capable of; how you were viewed by others; what was right and wrong; and whether you were okay or not okay.

In essence you had developed your Blueprint. This Blueprint informed you of what was expected of you and what you could expect from others and the world in which you lived.

## Repeat cycles

Sometimes, in childhood we have experiences that our child brains cannot make sense of because we do not have the knowledge, language or understanding to make sense of them. These events are sometimes traumatic and sometimes not, but the children this happens to will find themselves in repeat situations throughout their lives. The child and then the grown-up may experience Repeat Cycles in different situations but their storyline will remain the same, and this phenomenon will continue until they are able to make sense of and process it.

For example, if a child feels unloved by a parent (maybe because the parent is distracted by their own issues and is therefore emotionally unavailable), their child brain may not be able to make sense of it. They may think it is because they are faulty rather than because their parent has an issue. They may feel unlovable. As the child grows up they are likely to attract and be attracted to other people who they feel unloved by. They are likely to keep repeating this type of scenario unless they are able to understand and process the original event.

For a child, such an event would be like having a file that needs sorting into a filing cabinet, but when they get to the cabinet they find there isn't yet a corresponding section for the file to be placed in and they do not have the resources an adult may have to create a new section.

As the file is not processed or dealt with it remains unfiled and laying around and it continues to surface from time-to-time throughout a person's life in the form of uncomfortable feelings.

When the file (or unprocessed event and feelings) resurfaces it causes problems for the person. Clients tell me that rather than experiencing the discomfort of dealing with the issue contained in the file, they push it to the back of an imaginary shelf and live in the futile hope that it will not resurface.

Once the event *is* finally dealt with and processed, perhaps as an adult, a new section will be created in the figurative cabinet for the issue to be filed under and it ceases to resurface.

When you learned who you were by way of the Metaphorical Mirror (your parents showing you who you were) and your conditioning, you developed a Blueprint which has guided you through life.

It's rather like giving a dog a bad name. You generally expect that dog to grow into its name and be naughty. You have an expectation that the dog will behave badly and it will develop an expectation of itself that this is who it is. Of course this process is much more subtle within a family environment but the same principles apply.

Your Blueprint was developed by your Foundation and Framework and is filtered through your Wiring and Windows which gives you a unique understanding and perspective of yourself and the world around you. Repeat Cycles weave their way through your Blueprint.

**Velcro and Teflon Effects**

The Framework also creates a system which dictates what resonates with your brain and what doesn't.

For example if the messages you received in your Metaphorical Mirror indicated that you couldn't sing, that is what your brain was going accept. From that time on, every time you sang and people confirmed that your voice was not tuneful it would resonate with your brain and you could accept it. Whereas, if someone said your voice was tuneful (because they heard you in a different way or because you took singing lessons) your brain would reject the compliment.

These are the Velcro and Teflon Effects. Words either stick to you or slide off you as if you are wearing either a sticky Velcro suit or a non-stick Teflon suit.

**Velcro and Teflon Effects**

If you have low self-esteem and someone pays you a compliment you are likely to wear your Teflon suit as the compliment will slide right off you. However, if someone is mean to you it will be like wearing a Velcro suit as the words stick to you and you carry them around because they fit with your negative view of yourself. Much of this has happened on a subconscious level, out of your awareness. Until now.

As you grew you subconsciously internalised the messages from the Foundation of your parents and took the messages up into your Framework and beyond until you expected to be treated in certain ways.

As you got older and mixed with other children and other adults you behaved in ways that taught them how you expected to be treated. You, like many of us, probably had internal dialogues with yourself and spoke to yourself in the way you were spoken to as a child by your parents. This all further reinforces and cements your behaviours and conditioning.

Your genetics, your parents' messages, your interpretation of the messages, your Groundwork, Foundation and Framework were further weathered and adapted by your individual life experiences which may have included physical, sexual or emotional abuse, parents divorce, illness, financial hardship, accidents, death, abandonment, war, bullying, dyslexia, deafness, blindness, special needs, disability, neglect, even over protection or being overly praised.

Of course, your messages would also have been impacted by all the positive experiences you had, but as your subconscious is only interested in keeping you alive, the good experiences are not so relevant here.

By the time you finished primary school you subconsciously knew who you were and what was expected of you. Maybe you felt happy and carefree, loved, supported, nourished and nurtured, or maybe you felt afraid, less than, hopeless, sad or lost. All this, and millions of variations in between, were possible.

It is probably an impossible task to separate who you would have been without conditioning from who you are with it. Your conditioning became part of you and grew and developed with you. Much of your conditioning was and still is likely to be very helpful to you.

As well as the problem conditioning that negatively informed you of who you are, you probably received thousands of messages that kept you safe, such as look before you cross the road and eat your vegetables.

This process is not about negating all conditioning but more about exploring it and discovering what you wish to keep because it still serves you well and what you wish to discard because it's become a habit that no longer serves you well.

We have been given so many messages and expectations that it can be difficult to see who we truly are. This quote by Emily McDowell sums it up:

"Finding yourself is not really how it works. You aren't a ten dollar bill in last winter's coat pocket. You are also not lost. Your true self is right there, buried under cultural conditioning, other people's opinions, and inaccurate conclusions you drew as a kid that became your beliefs about who you are. 'Finding yourself' is actually returning to yourself. An unlearning, an excavation, a remembering who you were before the world got its hands on you."

In the past you may have felt uncomfortable asking for your own needs to be met and you went along with what others wanted to do in fear of getting it wrong and feeling humiliated. Now you can see that your choices and decisions are as valid and worthy as anyone else's.

**Questions:**

**Who did you become?**

1. Are you passive, aggressive, passive aggressive or assertive?

2. How were you praised as a child?

3. How were you punished as a child?

4. What strong beliefs do you hold?

5. How were you treated as a child if you were upset?

6. Describe yourself in three words?

7. What do you enjoy doing?

8. Did you experience any childhood trauma?

9. How do you behave when you are upset?

10. How do you treat other people?

# YOUR SMART BRAIN AND WIRING

At a tender age your Foundation was set, your Framework was in place and you were conditioned to think, feel and behave in certain ways. You were becoming hard wired (children's brains have been proven 'plastic and flexible' and therefore not hard wired but they are in the process of becoming so). From there on your Wiring informed you internally of who you were, what was expected of you, how others regarded you and how you should regard others. This Wiring was programmed by your Smart Brain.

Your Smart Brain was and is incredibly complex. It took all the information from your Foundation and Framework and came up with its own interpretations of the data.

Just like predictive text on a Smart Phone, your Smart Brain tried to predict the outcome of every situation before it had fully taken place based on the information it had stored at that time.

When you write a text message on a Smart Phone, predictive text guesses and finishes the word for you. You may start typing in the letters 'Foun' and before you finish typing, predictive text inserts the word 'Found'.

This creates efficiency by way of speed and lack of thought on the part of the phone user. Sometimes the word Found will be the correct word and sometimes the Smart Phone gets it wrong because the operator wanted to write Foundation or Foundry.

Something very similar happens with the Smart Brain when someone interacts with you, your Smart Brain gives you a meaning of the event based on the information you have received in life up to that point. Its aim is to be efficient and helpful, but in reality it can cause you to misinterpret what the communicator was trying to convey.

It's as if sometimes you become a Fortune Teller or Mind Reader predicting an outcome based on childhood understanding. If that understanding is incorrect, your assumptions or guesses will also be incorrect. For example, if the false messages you received as a young child caused you to believe: "I'm faulty," then your interpretation of some communications would be distorted by this belief. You may think that if someone tells you they are not happy, that it is somehow your fault and they are going to be angry with you. You have probably predicted a false outcome based on your false belief.

If a child is feeling unsafe because they live in a volatile or unpredictable environment they can subconsciously imagine their actions can control their parents' behaviours. If the way the child behaves coincides with parents being less scary, they will subconsciously hold onto this way of behaving and use it during future turmoil to control their environment. Of course, this is a false belief that helps the child feel safe. However, your Smart Brain would interpret your childhood belief as fact. As you grew and developed you would continue to believe this information and grow into a person who subconsciously thinks: "If I please others, they will treat me well." It's as if you believed you could control people's behaviour and therefore predict the outcome.

The more you use specific words when texting the quicker your phone recognises them and predicts their future use. The more you use a false belief or distorted view the easier it becomes for your Smart Brain to recognise it as familiar and predict future events based on this inaccurate information.

It goes back to the Traffic Jam, where the individual drivers each have their unique reaction to the situation. The event is what it is, and yet all the drivers create their own interpretations of the event depending on their internal understandings and viewpoints (Wiring and Windows).

It becomes even more difficult to communicate effectively when the speaker also has their own interpretation of the listener's reaction to their words.

No wonder we default to only experiencing the world from our own point-of-view with little consideration for how someone else may be understanding it.

For example, suppose a good friend failed to return a person's calls. An insecure person with questionable Wiring may jump to the conclusion that their friend no longer liked them and that they must have done something to upset them. Due to this type of negative mind reading they may feel rejected and upset. When the friend eventually calls, the insecure person might not answer because they predict that their friend is going to be annoyed with them. The result is that they fall out with their good friend.

In the same situation a secure person may feel confident that they have done nothing to upset their friend and would consider that there must be other reasons why their calls had not been returned, such as their phone not working properly or because they are busy. Due to this line of thinking they remain feeling neutral and do not predict negative future scenarios.

Just as well all this happens on a subconscious level, out of our awareness, so we don't have to think about it. Our poor conscious brains would certainly experience overload otherwise.

**The Subconscious**

The subconscious (also called the unconscious) makes up more than 90% of our psyche and our conscious mind is less than 10%. If you think of the psyche as an iceberg, the tiny portion sticking up above the water is the conscious mind that deals with willpower, decisions, critical thinking, planning, short-term memory, and logical thinking. The huge part under the water represents the subconscious which controls beliefs, emotions, habits, values, long term memory, bodily functions, imagination, intuition and resistance to change (Snagging).

Your conscious thoughts and actions are literally the things you think about with awareness, like deciding what to wear, writing a shopping list, cooking a meal, in fact anything you do when you are mentally present. Your unconscious is out of your awareness, and controls things like your muscles holding your head up while you read this book, dreaming, or behaviours you exhibit and have no idea that you do.

Your breathing is interesting. Up until now you have not been thinking about how you breathe, and you have been breathing unconsciously. Now that I've mentioned it, the fact that you are breathing has moved up into your awareness. If you now take three really deep breathes and feel that breath at the back of your throat on the first breath, then in your lungs on the second and then deep down in your stomach on the third, you will most definitely be breathing consciously.

## The Iceberg
### Conscious

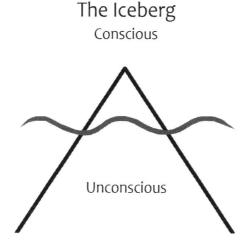

Unconscious

Your Smart Brain mainly operates within your unconscious. This is where your conditioning, your beliefs, your view of yourself and others and your habits reside. Your Foundation, Framework and your subsequent internal network of Wiring are all operating at a subconscious level.

When your Groundwork, Foundation and Framework are secure and solid the resulting Wiring reflects this because your subconsciously-operated Smart Brain works accurately. However, when some of your building materials are questionable and your builders received poor quality training  your Wiring tends to short-circuit because your Smart Brain misinterprets information.

Just as predictive text sometimes gets the meaning wrong, so does your Smart Brain. Sometimes our Wiring has broken connections and so the messages become confused. What if the messages you received from your parents were misinformed? Perhaps their Wiring was questionable and this has impacted on your Wiring.

What if the Metaphorical Mirror they held up showed you  you were unlovable, bad or faulty by way of their distorted view and this wasn't who you actually were at all?

Many of my clients tell me earnestly that they think they were bad children and deserved to be punished in the ways they were. They say they wouldn't have been smacked so severely if they weren't so naughty or they must have acted too provocatively around uncle when they were eight therefore encouraging his attentions.

The messages they received were that they were bad, not because they were bad, but because they perceived that they were told verbally and non-verbally that they were bad. They internalised these messages and truly believed that they were bad people. Can you imagine having Wiring that reinforces that belief throughout your life?

Make no mistake that the child who is labelled bad was never born bad. The child was told they were bad and lived out their life script (or Blueprint) in accordance with that label.

Simultaneously, while your Foundation, Framework and Wiring was developing, your Windows (or filters) were also developing. The Metaphorical Mirror your parents held up to show you who you were was then being reinforced by your own experiences in life a) because you tend to attract what is expected of you and what you expect for yourself and b) because even if it doesn't match your Blueprint, your filter will interpret it in a way that best fits your expectation. Which takes you back to predictive text and Velcro (accepting what fits and negating what doesn't).

When you look at who you are, you see who your parents told you you were. How correct was that information? Do you want to believe them? Do you have no say in who you actually are?

The bottom line is that you can decide to be who they've told you you are or you can decide to be who you actually are. Deciding to rewire yourself is the first step towards conscious change.

Until you have awareness of what you do and why, it's a bit like repeatedly falling down the same holes in the road and not even seeing the holes. Then you become aware of the holes and you are initially still compelled to fall down them. The next stage is when you can see the holes and choose to walk around them. Eventually you can choose to walk in a different direction. This is when the rewiring is complete.

You have a right to ask questions and challenge traditions; to ask for help if you need assistance and you have every right to learn by making mistakes.

You feel empowered to act now, and you know no one has a right to place you in uncomfortable situations.

You find yourself expecting to be respected and you respect those around you. You may find yourself spending more time with people who love and support you and you have every right to spend less time with anybody who puts you down or repeatedly criticises you.

Every day you become interested to find you are speaking up for yourself and realising how easy it is and how good it feels to have your voice heard and respected.

**Questions:**

**What does your Smart Brain keep repeating?**

1. What are your habitual ways of thinking, feeling or behaving?

2. What similar problem situations do you find yourself in?

3. What do you complain to your friends and family about?

4. Do you do feel appreciated for what you do for others?

5. Do you feel unloved, unlovable, bad or at fault?

6. Do you think people are out to get you or that you should get them first?

7. Do you feel that others are more deserving than you or that you are equal?

8. Do you feel that others are more capable of dealing with problems than you are?

9. Do you speak to yourself within your internal dialogue in a kind or harsh manner?

10. Are you superstitious, such as believing that walking under ladders brings bad luck?

# YOUR PERSPECTIVE
# YOUR WINDOWS

Psychiatrist Carl Jung said: "It all depends on how we look at things, and not how they are in themselves."

As already mentioned your family history, parents' messages and conditioning cause you to view yourself and others in a particular way. This is your filter through which you make sense of what is happening around you and within you.

This filter is like being given a pair of glasses as a small child through which you will always see a similar perspective. In the analogy of your Tower these are the Windows through which you see out of and into your Tower. How cloudy, distorted or clear your Windows are will determine your view.

Your Windows developed concurrently with your Wiring and they overlap considerably. They are interlinked and interwoven by your unique Smart Brain. Your Windows give you a view of yourself and the world around you based on your Smart Brain's programming. Your Smart Brain's programming is reinforced and enhanced by the view from your Windows.

Your subconscious will pass all information through the filter of your Windows to see whether it fits your Blueprint or not. For instance, if the information is a remark about you and it does not fit your view of yourself it will be as if you are wearing your Teflon suit and the words will slide off you, but if the remark is what you believe about yourself and therefore fits your view of yourself it will stick to you as if you are wearing your Velcro suit.

Sometimes your subconscious Windows will actually twist the information to enable it to fit. For example, if someone pays you a compliment and you have a low view of yourself, you may see their remark as a sarcastic insult rather than the intended compliment because that fits your Blueprint and will therefore enable it to stick like Velcro.

In other words the glass in your Windows distorts so you see things in a way that makes sense to your brain's Wiring, regardless of whether it is fact in reality.

### I'm okay, you're okay

The messages you received from your parents when they showed you the Metaphorical Mirror will have a direct impact on your Windows.

Your perspective through your Windows will determine how you think about yourself and others and this will determine how you feel about yourself and others. You will end up in one of several scenarios: a) I'm okay and others are okay; b) I'm okay and others are not okay; c) I'm not okay and others are okay; and d) I'm not okay and others are not okay.

This way of categorisation was introduced by psychiatrist Eric Berne in his 1950s theory of Transactional Analysis, or TA for short, which looked at how we interact with ourselves and others. It was later simplified by Frank Ernst who created the 'I'm okay, you're okay' matrix.

'I'm okay and you're okay' is the perspective of a secure, assertive person with healthy self-esteem. The other three views are from insecure passive, aggressive, or passive-aggressive people with low self-esteem.

These various viewpoints will control your way of thinking, and as described later, your thinking directly determines how you feel. Your feelings are always valid. How you feel is how you feel and no one can rightfully argue differently. However, the thoughts that caused those feelings can be inaccurate (depending on your Smart Brain and Window distortions), therefore effectively tricking you into feeling something that is not true.

When you were born you were an innocent, lovely little baby. Your Foundation and your subsequent Framework was affected by how your parents spoke to you and treated you. For example, if they told you that you were so loved and special and they behaved accordingly, you were unlikely to form the feeling and then the belief that you were unlovable and unworthy.

Sometimes your feelings are so strong that you believe that the thought or the meaning you have placed on the event that led to them must be true. This kind of distortion leads to you gathering false information and forming an incorrect meaning (or False Belief), just like predictive text getting it wrong.

As a baby you didn't question the way you were spoken to. You simply took the words and tones of these great Beings you depended upon for survival as true. Your parents told you who you were and you believed it. Even if you think differently as a logical adult, you are highly likely to still believe these messages on a deep internal level.

You have every right to express your emotions and to feel emotional because all your emotions are valid. You can now see that you are equal to others and have as much right as anyone else to be treated fairly and with respect.

**Mixed messages**

Sometimes the messages you received from your parents might have contradicted one another, so your Window glass could have been distorted and also confusingly cloudy.

The following is a true story from a client. As a child, she wanted to do what her parents asked of her, because she had been conditioned to do as she was told or face the consequences.

She believed that her parents had taught her that if she got a toy out to play with and her sister then joined in the game, it was up to her sister to put the toy away. When my client, aged about eight, put this into practise, her father bellowed at her for not putting the toy away herself. She back-chatted him due to feeling the injustice of the situation. She had been chastised for doing what she believed would keep her safe from punishment and then further punished for standing up for herself.

She had tried to follow the rules as she saw them but then her father appeared to change them. The effect this, and further reinforcement had, was that her Windows became a  filter of self-doubt. She no longer trusted her view of herself or the world around her.

This type of conditioning resulted in her Wiring and Windows showing her inaccurate information. It manifested into her feeling insecure because she would have thoughts like: "I always get it wrong. I think I'm doing the right thing, but others always know better than me," which leads to the matrix style of 'I'm not okay, but you're okay'.

**False Beliefs**

False beliefs cause a distorted view through your Window. If the view you hold of yourself is incorrect, the view you believe others hold of you is incorrect and the view you have of other people can also be incorrect.

These incorrect views create False Beliefs (or thoughts) and produce corresponding feelings (your feelings are always valid, but sometimes the thoughts on which they are based are incorrect).

Babies, toddlers, and children are vulnerable and helpless. They do not have the knowledge, strength, independence or power to stand up to adults. In fact they are at the mercy of the adults around them and are developing as a result of these adults' actions and messages.

Let's look at a baby who was fostered at just a few months old. He has no knowledge of what is happening. He simply feels. He feels that the person who he was meant to stay with (his mother) is no longer there. He doesn't understand why. He bonds with his foster carer and is then adopted by another family at the age of six.

He doesn't know how the system works or about the process; all he feels is that someone else who was supposed to love him has given him away and rejected him. He feels abandoned and this becomes his Window design on his Blueprint.

Is it any wonder he grows up unable to trust others; feeling unworthy of love and fearing abandonment, despite having secure foster and adoptive parents?

His Wiring was short circuited early on and his Windows were distorted by situations that had nothing to do with who he was. He felt abandoned, so he thought and then believed he must be unlovable.

Then there's the child who lives in a volatile household where mum and dad argue, shout and fight. They both drink and take drugs and one minute they appear loving and predictable and the next they are scary and aggressive. This child has been born into a war zone and has no control over the situation.

The only thing the child can control is their self, so they watch for clues; they learn to second-guess or mind-read situations; they believe that if they act in a certain way or go through a certain routine (like counting or turning round three times) they can somehow affect what is happening around them.

You can maybe imagine how this affects their Wiring and Windows.

The child has no control, so they pretend they have control and their imagination keeps them feeling safer or they find other situations which they can control e.g. restricting food. Sometimes the only control a child has is by believing that they are somehow responsible for the chaos they are living in. The child will always blame their self rather than their parents. It makes sense, because if it was their parents' fault the child would have no control over what was happening and that might be unbearable.

How often does a child think: "Oh yeah mum and dad are fighting because dad is an aggressive alcoholic and mum keeps having affairs?" Rarely. The child is more likely to turn it in on their self. In the child's mind their parents are the gods who love them and want what's best for them. If parents are bad towards a child it must be the child's fault. If the parents are bad to one another it must be the child's fault. If the parents get divorced it must be the child's fault. The child has no control over their environment so they learn ways to feel in control and therefore safer such as believing it is their fault. Of course, this is make-believe in their subconscious imaginations.

These types of situations shape the child's perspective (or Windows).  They often form negative views of their self  and of the world around them. If you've received negative information about yourself it makes sense that your view of yourself and the world would also be negative.

This can lead to thinking (and therefore feeling) that your opinion is not worthy and  that other people can't be trusted  either (I'm not okay and you're not okay); or you can feel that your opinion is correct and others are wrong (I'm okay, you're not okay) or it can lead you to believe that your perspective is wrong and other people's views are always correct (I'm not okay, you're okay).

You have a right to put your own needs first especially if other people are taking advantage of you. And now you can see that those old feelings that stopped you from being assertive, confident and respected were given to you by people who were afraid of losing control.

Have you ever met somebody who has a thoroughly negative view. You ask them: "How are you today?" and their sad, resigned face says: "Same old stuff, different day." Any suggestion you make to brighten their life is met with: "I suppose I could, but......," and they'll list all the reasons why they can't.

They say a negative person will find a problem for every solution. When someone has negative conditioning, they think negatively and this causes them to feel negative and this can affect their behaviour in negative ways. It's no surprise when they get negative results and of course, this reinforces their negative thoughts.

**Questions:**

**How do you see yourself and others?**

1. Where are you in your family's pecking order?

2. Do you feel content with who you are (I'm okay)?

3. Do you feel content with how other people are (you're okay)?

4. Do you like or love yourself?

5. Does the world feel safe to you or do you feel anxious about it?

6. How do other people behave towards you?

7. Do you feel that some people love you?

8. What do people like or love about you?

9. Do you trust other people?

10. Do you feel like an outsider among your friends, colleagues or family?

# EARLY YEARS COPING /ADAPTING YOUR SCAFFOLDING

As we've seen in the last chapter children live in environments over which they have little or no control. They cannot change what is around them so they change themselves. They adapt in order to cope with the environment they find themselves living in. In the Tower analogy these coping methods are the Scaffolding. Children use two types of Scaffolding: control and avoidance.

The few things a baby or small child can control (although these would not be conscious actions) are what goes into their body and what comes out of it. By refusing food or refusing to poop the child has some kind of control and this can help their subconscious feel safer. Whether or not they will go to sleep when the parent or carer wants them to can be another form of control.

Your subconscious has one primary function and that is to keep you alive. The safer it feels the more likely it is to repeat behaviours.

For the parents these behaviours might be frustrating and annoying. They may cause them to think: "Why is my child doing this?" or "what is my child trying to tell me here?" but often parents are engaged in their own thoughts, feelings and behaviours and are less likely to respond with such relaxed curiosity.

They may interpret  the child as deliberately misbehaving, so more control is put in place by the parent by way of criticism, chastisement, bribery, or looks of disappointment and disapproval. These  reinforce the child's belief about themselves, which may be that they are bad or faulty. Maybe it's a way of the resourceful child getting their parent to take control, which serves as a boundary in which the child feels safer. No attention is bad attention.

Another behaviour of young children is screaming and thrashing which has an element of controlling the parent, but also acts as an avoidant method to smother uncomfortable feelings.

By the time the child reaches primary school age they may be feeling insecure within the Wiring and Windows they have already developed. Their Brickwork is now developing around their Framework and already cracks may be showing.

If things at home were rocky and unpredictable, being thrust into a new environment such as school with a ratio of one adult to up to thirty children is unlikely to help matters, especially if the child feels abandoned by their parents.

When a child feels unsafe they adapt themselves in order to cope with their uncomfortable feelings.

Like so many parents, mine had no rule-book on how to bring up a child and probably parented me as they were themselves parented, some of it helpful and some of it not. I'm certain I did the same with my children.

When I was very young I was 'clingy' and would hide behind my mum's skirt if someone came to the door, or so I was told. My mum was so concerned by my shy behaviour that she asked the doctor's advice. He recommended that she go to work and leave me at home in the care of my dad who worked nights. The separation was hoped to stop me being so needy of my mum. Of course, it caused me to feel more insecure. I remember sitting at the table as a 3-year-old with my imaginary friends, playing Lego while dad got on with his grown-up stuff; namely, building a bathroom in our house.

I was safe and he knew where I was, but I was lonely while he was busy. So the way I coped was to create imaginary friends. This was my avoidant Scaffolding. I could talk to them and avoid feeling lonely.

Children use their creative imaginations to invent friends and pretend scenarios in order to feel safe. These coping methods help them avoid and control their reality.

**Other types of Early Years Scaffolding:**

**Magical Thinking**

Magical Thinking can be imaginatively developed by the child so they feel that a behaviour or set of behaviours (such as counting or turning around three times) will have some power over their situation. It gives them a sense of control.

Some people will not walk on the cracks of the pavements in order to avoid something bad happening, or they'll turn around and spit after walking under a ladder to negate the bad luck.

It appears that childhood Magical Thinking could be the forerunner of adult superstitions. I have known children go through complex routines of head-turning from one side to the other in order to believe that the following day would be okay. I've known children rewind songs and videos repeatedly until they felt that they had done it enough to prevent bad things from happening.

Obsessive Compulsive Disorder in later years all starts somewhere. People don't usually start obsessively checking doors and switching lights on and off in a sequence without some form of early learned adaptive-behaviours.

**Objectifying**

Some children have toys or objects that they truly love because they become like a mother-figure to them. As long as that toy or object is with them they feel some comfort and security as if mum was there.

As mentioned before, your earliest bonds with your primary carers (often mum) impacts on your Blueprint. This bond creates the part of your Blueprint which relates to how you interpret relationships and interact within them. This part of the Blueprint is also known in counselling terms as your Attachment Style and is developed within the first 18 months of your life.

A child may have an insecure Attachment Style because their mum was emotionally unavailable or always on her phone, and the child felt alone. This child may find security in a physical object such as a toy or blanket. If they have an insecure Attachment Style they may be more likely to suffer distrust; be emotionally distant; fear being single, or 'parent' their partner in later life. They also tend to become adults with lower self-esteem. A child who has a secure Attachment Style because their mum consistently showed them unconditional positive regard, usually has trusting, lasting relationships as an adult and healthy self-esteem.

**Dissociation**

Another way of avoiding an otherwise emotionally overwhelming experience is to dissociate or daydream. Some children find themselves locking their vision and thoughts onto an inanimate object in order to be distracted from the reality of what is happening to them. This can enable them to blank or block out a traumatic situation.

Others daydream about being somewhere totally different to where they actually are and build up that imagined place to block out the bad feelings they are experiencing.

This is an instance of children unknowingly using Cognitive Behavioural Therapy to replace bad feelings with good ones. What you think and imagine impacts on how you feel. Think nice thoughts and feel good. Think unpleasant or worrying thoughts and feel bad.

## Parenting the parent

Some children actually appear to parent their parents. This may begin when the child feels that the unease around them is their fault and that their behaviour could change their environment. In order to feel in control they begin to take responsibility for their parent's emotions. In this role-reversal the child parents their parent. If mum is tearful and appears vulnerable the child may feel the need to comfort and reassure her. If dad is volatile or irresponsible the child may feel the need to take responsibility.

## Hyper-vigilance

This is almost the opposite of dissociation. The child may become hyper-vigilant and learn to notice everything that is going on in order to feel they have some control over the chaotic world they live in. They notice the way a door is closed or a key is placed on a shelf and hundreds of other tiny clues that may help them predict any forthcoming danger. This enables them to second-guess what others need and by doing so they can fulfil that need and prevent the danger, or recognise the impending danger and take cover; an exhausting form of feeling safe and in control.

## Protesting

Protesting, screaming, pleading and sulking are all forms of behaviour that children learn will often get their needs met by wearing down their parents. The feelings of guilt or exasperation experienced by the grown-up often leads to them giving in to the expressive child.

These methods of adapting in order to cope are internalised into the child's Wiring and repeated throughout life. These messages are added to the child's Blueprint of who they are and what is expected of them. Time and again I work with clients who, into their middle age and beyond, exhibit behaviours that served them well as children trying to cope with difficult surroundings, but in their adult lives cause them distress. One of the most common is the child parent-pleaser who develops into the People Pleaser.

## People Pleasing

Children are by nature egocentric (or narcissistic) and therefore believe that everything happens because of them. This is why a child can learn to feel like they can control the environment around them by their actions. Due to the process of conditioning, they learn that when they do something helpful they are praised and when they do something wrong they are scolded. In other words when they are good, good things happen, and when they are bad, bad things happen. It makes sense therefore that if mum and dad are fighting, which is a bad thing, the child might believe (subconsciously) that if they are good the fight will stop.

The child adapts their self to become whatever is needed in order to create a safer feeling place. When the child notices that their actions have created desired results they continue to repeat their behaviour. This 'good outcome' might just be an illusion and appear to work because of coincidence, but the child-brain processes this information as truth and believes they have actually changed their parents' behaviour by changing theirs. Because the child idolises their parents, the child cannot process the idea of their parents being at fault so it must be the child's fault. This enables the child to feel in control and therefore safer. Of course this simply adds to the illusion, but the belief helps the child live within difficult surroundings. The child's behaviour becomes a habit and this habit develops into becoming a People Pleaser in later life.

The fear that holds them in this habit is that people may not like them, people may feel hurt or bad things may happen if they change their behaviour.

**Questions:**

**How did you adapt and cope as a child?**

1. What was your home environment like?

2. Can you remember any tense or difficult situations?

3. What was it like to be you in your home?

4. Were you shy or outgoing?

5. Did you feel afraid, angry, safe or sad at home?

6. Did you have any Magical Thinking?

7. Did you behave in certain ways to feel safe?

8. How did you behave in order to get noticed?

9. What was your parents' response to your behaviours?

10. Did you have a special toy that you kept close by you?

# TEENAGE YEARS
# YOUR BUILDING INSPECTORS
# STEP BACK

Your Wiring and Windows are firmly in place and the Brickwork has been forming around your Framework in a unified pattern pre-determined in those earliest years as your Blueprint.

The pattern of your Brickwork has been repeated daily for years now and your teenage Smart Brain is well established and goes unquestioned by you.

The way it is, is the way it has always been for you. It is your normal. By the time you reach your early teens your parents have taught you everything they need you to know and now you are continuing to reinforce what you have learned and internalised with your own (copied and conditioned) behaviours.

They have held up that Metaphorical Mirror for many years now and you have been well and truly conditioned into knowing who they think you should be based on their Foundations.

You have been told, taught and shown, and have developed learned behaviours and coping mechanisms.

All this has been continuously reinforced by your parents and then internally by your Smart Brain using your Wiring and Windows to process incoming information.

At this point the way you see things is totally normal to you and therefore you would have no reason to consider that anyone else would see things any differently from you. Up until now anybody who was worth listening to (mainly your parents) have shared your beliefs and values (because they gave them to you).

Your world until now has been fairly closed and restricted to your family system. Their Foundation affected your Foundation, and you would have added some refinements of your own as you became influenced by teachers, peers, social media etc.

Now life becomes a bit more exciting. Your Building Inspectors (parents) take a step back, and you discover some freedom as you start adding your own details to your Tower. Your parents become less of an influence and friends become much more significant. A teenager's behaviour will be greatly determined by the need to gain approval from and to avoid disapproval from their peers (rather than from their parents).

Your friendship groups broaden and become more important; your independence increases; you are bigger and more resourceful; you spend less time with your parents; and with the onset of hormones come new wonderful feelings around love and sex, as well as confusing mood swings, altered sleeping habits and changing body image.

You may play sport, smoke weed or study hard (or do all of these), but your subconscious autopilot is still using your Blueprint as its guide. You have internalised your parents' teachings and developed your own internal Building Inspector.

As your world expands you begin to notice that what has always been normal to you is not normal for everyone else. The way you have been conditioned to live is not the same as for everyone else. You discover that different people have been conditioned in different ways and they do not all hold the same values as you.

**Roast dinners on Sunday**

Ever since you were born you have been moulded, conditioned, and brainwashed in thousands of different ways. Maybe one of those ways was that every Sunday your family had roast dinner.

This is true of your family and therefore you believe it would be true of all families. Why wouldn't you? You've had no reason to question it or consider that there could be an alternative. Until now.

How it has been, is as it is, and how it should be, must be and ought to be because your parents and family deemed it so.

Imagine that you are 13-years-old and your friend suggests hanging out with them on Sunday. You would expect your friend's family to have roast dinner and might also expect them to invite you along. A reasonable assumption.

On the day in question you have it somewhere in your head that your friend's family will at some point call you through to the kitchen for roast dinner. It doesn't happen. Your friend suggests putting a pizza in the oven. This is your first taste of something not being as you assumed it would be. You may a) think your friend is really weird; b) feel confused; or c) embrace the difference without judgement. Of course, your reaction would depend on your Wiring and Windows.

As you progress through your teens you begin to realise that all the information you have been told, shown, or taught is not the only way. It can be challenged, and you begin to question and doubt your parents' beliefs and values. You may begin to realise that your grown-ups are not gods to be idolised, but ordinary people with strengths and weaknesses of their own.

You have walked the same path for many years. This path was created for you and you have blindly followed its track every day. Now you have forged a new path of your own creation and every day that you walk this path it becomes stronger, clearer and more defined. One day soon, the old path will lose its definition and faded away.

**Questions:**

**How were your teenage years?**

1. What was normal for you?

2. What did you and your parents disagree on?

3. How did you rebel?

4. How did you change as a teenager?

5. Were you teased (bullied) at all – at school or at home?

6. How would your parents and your friends have described you?

7. How would you describe yourself as a teenager?

8. How did you spend your time?

9. What did you do without your parents' knowledge?

10. What particular events come to mind when you think of high school?

# TEENAGE YEARS
# COPING/REBELLING
# YOUR SCAFFOLDING

Pushing the boundaries set by your parents is a natural progression from child to adult. The blinkers fall away to a certain extent as you begin to discover that everything you have known is not quite as it had previously appeared. The safety of certainty begins to crack and life feels scary as well as exciting.

Add to this the hormonal explosion erupting from within you, your adult size, intelligence, and communication skills, and it is no surprise that war breaks out. The teenager may challenge their parents' beliefs or they may challenge their peers as they try to uphold their parents' instilled values. Either way there is often internal and external turmoil.

Due to hormones and body changes teenagers can look physically like adults but, mentally, and maturity and intelligence-wise they are still young and, for example, have child-like impulse control. This fuels some of the challenges faced by teenagers such as parents expecting them to be grown-up and look after their self.

If you now take an objective look at your Tower you can assess the quality of the Groundwork which affected the quality of your Foundation; the structure of your Foundation which formed your Framework; and how all the above influenced your Wiring, Windows and Brickwork.

Until now you may never have questioned your Tower's design or the materials used. It may be as if it just rose from the ground without any real thought. And this is fairly accurate due to our behaviours mainly being unconscious.

When you were a teenager was probably the first time you had any conscious awareness that you were separate from your parents and that you could have different thoughts and opinions from them.

You might have realised that although you were heavily influenced by your family, you were becoming more influenced by other things outside of them, such as peers and politics. This could have caused conflict within you.

For the first time, your head was excited by new and convincing information and yet your heart still held on to conditioned beliefs and values.

You are equal to all other humans and as such have a right to share your thoughts and feelings with others as they too enjoy sharing their thoughts and feelings with you. Now you can see that you deserve to be appreciated as you refuse to be taken for granted.

If you had a secure base you would likely hold assertive values which would allow you to conclude that although your world was different from others, that was okay. You would be able to see the other person's perspective and viewpoint and not be afraid to either change your mind upon reflection or stick with your original conditioned opinion without putting other people down (I'm okay, you're okay).

If your teenage base was insecure you would likely show passive, aggressive or passive-aggressive behaviour in regards to other people's differences. Your inner turmoil would likely be greater as you grappled with being afraid to challenge another person's opinion (I'm not okay, you're okay); or needed to manipulate the person in order to get your view heard without fear of recriminations (I'm not okay, you're not okay); or you may simply have punched the person who disagreed with you (I'm okay, you're not okay).

Exacerbating this situation is the teenagers brain development. Teenagers are typically more impulsive and drawn to risk-taking. During this stage of life the prefrontal cortex of the brain (the area that does the rational thinking) is slower to develop. This part of the brain generally catches up between the ages of 20-25.

If you were inclined towards an insecure base your already slightly crumbling Tower might have begun to sway uncontrollably during your teenage years, and as you desperately tried to regain control or avoid the impending disaster, you may have reached for Scaffolding. Your teenage Scaffolding had the same purpose and was used in a similar way as that of your childhood coping mechanisms; however, the types of avoidance and control became more advanced.

Some teenage Avoidant-Scaffolding includes drinking alcohol, taking drugs, self-harming, over-studying, over-exercising, gambling, sex addiction, gaming and looking after others rather than their self.

Some Control-Scaffolding would include food control (often leading to eating disorders), set routines or behaviours (often leading to Obsessive Compulsive Disorder), physical or emotional bullying (leading to future abusive relationships), self-harming, People Pleasing, stealing, over-exercising, over-studying.

Notice that some forms of Scaffolding cleverly fit into both categories. Self-harm may help ease the internal pain by distraction, thereby avoiding it, and could also create a desirable reaction from others, which is a type of manipulation or control.

All these methods may be helpful in the short-term because, however bad they appear, they are all Scaffolding, and Scaffolding can prevent or at least delay the teen from collapse, breakdown and even suicide.

These are tough years for all concerned, teens and their parents. For a teenager, what is most helpful is loving understanding, gentle guidance and support, and clear but slightly flexible boundaries.

However, what they often receive is punishment, anger, cold shouldering, bribery, too strict or too relaxed or inconsistent boundaries causing a whole lot more Tower wobbling.

**Suicidal Feelings**

People generally don't want to talk about suicidal thoughts and feelings, which is all the more reason to bring them out in the open.

It is said that: "Suicidal thoughts have helped many a person cope with the darkest of nights."

This may seem like a very strange thing to say, but for some people, when life feels overwhelming and too much to tolerate, the thought of suicide is a comfort. It feels like an escape route when there seems to be nowhere else to go. It can feel like there is a back door which they don't expect to use, but just knowing it is there can give someone enough strength or hope to carry on a bit longer.

I have heard elderly people admit that they have repeatedly considered that back door since their teenage years and planned how it might feel to walk through it.

Of course, for other people that escape route does feel like the only alternative to the emotional pain, numbness or nothingness that they experience, and they will leave through it.

This is not a selfish act, but an only way out of hell for them.

It is often through not wanting to hurt family and friends that may lead suicidal people to remain in a living hell for years.

## Birds leave the nest

I have a theory that the fraught times when teens challenge their parents helps to develop a young adult's independence and enables them to gain a sense of self and separateness from their parents which encourages them to leave home.

Although the teen may love their parents they may discover that they do not agree with some of the behaviours and restrictions that are placed on them.

On the flip side, the parents can feel out-of-control (and are having to erect their own Scaffolding) and as much as they love their child they may no longer recognise them and will find it difficult to tolerate their behaviours.

And so the two do part. Once this natural process of the bird flying free from the nest is complete, relationships often soon repair. Young adults begin seeing their parents as ordinary people like everyone else.

My daughter, psychologist Kayleigh Skene, said: "I totally agree. When I interviewed homeless teens for my dissertation, most of them said that they were thrown out or chose to leave home because of conflict with parents, but ever since leaving home their relationships had begun to improve and they found that they appreciated rather than resented the time they spent together."

This parting often leads to the Tower stabilising and the Scaffolding falling away on its own. The young adult is then in a position to start their own creative Brickwork without their Building Inspector constantly looking over their shoulder.

They have now developed an internal Building Inspector, which means they subconsciously filter their choices through their parents' preferences.

So, ironically, it doesn't matter if they consciously use different coloured bricks from their parents; subconsciously they are following their original Blueprint.

It's rather like when you leave the house on a cold day and you hear a parental voice in your head saying something like: "Make sure you wrap up warm," so you grab a coat.

**Questions:**

**How did you cope as a teenager?**

1. How did you feel as a teenager?

2. Did you feel conflicted about any restrictions your parents placed on you?

3. What methods did you use to feel better?

4. How did they make you feel?

5. How did you feel later or the next day?

6. Did you use mainly controlling or avoidant behaviours?

7. How did your parents react to your methods of coping?

8. What messages did they metaphorically send you?

9. How did your Scaffolding help you?

10. Were you keen to leave home or reluctant?

# GROWN-UP LIFE
# YOUR BRICKWORK

The young adult may or may not leave home and live an independent life. Those who don't may not be able to do this for many reasons as previously discussed – beliefs, thoughts, feelings, behaviours, expectations, fears etc, or due to having limited money or employment.

**Doing too much for teenagers**

In my counselling room I see more and more young adults who suffer with anxiety and depression. When they tell me about their upbringing, rather than telling me how difficult their childhood was, they report that they had the best parents ever.

They were given every opportunity to pursue what they wanted to do, had their food prepared and put in front of them and were not expected to help around the house. Often their parents would still be waking them up in the morning with tea and toast, turning their televisions off for them at night and making sure their phones and gadgets were plugged in for charging.

These well-meaning parents would often make a phone call or speak to teachers on behalf of their teenager so their child didn't have to endure the difficult feelings of fear, disappointment or disapproval that they perhaps experienced as teenagers.

The adults' behaviour may be a direct result of over-compensating for how they felt when they had to endure these difficult feelings, but the knock-on effect is that the child feels unable and afraid to do things for themselves. Their parent has unwittingly disempowered them.

(This parental behaviour may also be due to being the grandchildren or great grandchildren of those who experienced the hardships of World War Two or other difficult times in other countries. Those times of constraint, minimal resource and struggle may have caused each future generation to compensate by providing more comfort for their children when they could.)

Imagine, for instance, that a mother always cooks for their child and never encourages them to prepare their own meals. The parent may think: "I'm a good parent. I provide a healthy meal for my child and this gives them more time to do other things."

The child then approaches the age of 18 and has never had to prepare their own meals. The expectation is that they are going to go to university or out to work and fend for themselves. But they've never done it, so it is terrifying for them.

It's like a child being in a boat with their parents every day for 18 years and the parents not teaching the child how to row. "It's okay, I'll do it for you." Maybe you want to protect them and save their aching arms or you think they'll row incorrectly or too slowly, or you fear they may lose an oar.

The result is that they have little idea how to row and they develop thoughts like: "I won't be any good at that" or "that will be too difficult for me" or "I'll mess up and my parents will be disappointed in me".

These thoughts develop into feelings of incapability, helplessness and hopelessness, which can sometimes lead to anxiety and depression.

The child is nearing 18 and is petrified at the prospect of being put in their own boat. Anxiety is overwhelming. Their sense of hopelessness feeds into this. Because they are so scared they refuse to leave their parents' boat and because they see no way of getting in their own boat they see no future for themselves and so they become depressed. What a horrible place to be.

It's like having a terrible fear of heights and being told to climb to the top of a 30ft ladder. Much less scary to take smaller steps one rung at a time over a period of time.

Children who are supported while they learn to experience uncomfortable feelings and to overcome obstacles develop confidence and the knowledge that they are capable of dealing with situations as they arise.

If a child is not allowed or is sheltered from experiencing difficult feelings and activities they become disempowered and afraid.

Parents who allow their children to make some mistakes and then support them to overcome the difficulty may be more valuable to the child than wrapping them in cotton wool and protecting them from minor harms.

Those young adults who are empowered and motivated to leave home are able to carve out a life for themselves. They will start work, find accommodation, begin relationships and maybe start a family. Some may travel and some may not, but all the time they are building their own Towers they are building on the Foundation their parents provided and with a Blueprint which is unique to them.

As a grown-up we may become busy and focused on that next piece of life, next house, next relationship, next child, next job, next holiday. We may be well and truly on the hamster wheel of life that turns so quickly that we don't stop to think.

Life can flourish and life can wane. Some people can go on for years in contentment and some people notice cracks appearing in their Tower very rapidly.

Some people live their entire lives without appearing to suffer too much difficulty with their mental health, while others start to wobble at the slightest change in circumstances. Maybe this is due to the security of their Foundation and maybe this is due to life being random in who suffers what.

One result seems generalised throughout. If you suffer one of life's blows you will emotionally revert to your child-feeling self.

I often see clients who were able to temporarily divert from their childhood Blueprint  and appear to have transformed into a secure and assertive adult. Then a divorce, death or redundancy, rocked their core and their childhood vulnerability was shaken to the surface.

In the 1940s, American psychologist Abraham Maslow said that people prioritised certain needs, such as basic survival needs and only once these needs were met were they motivated to move on to achieve other needs.

Basic survival needs include food, water, warmth and rest.

He believed that only once  these survival needs were met  would we be able to prioritise our basic needs of safety.

Once we felt safe our psychological needs of feeling that we belong and are loved could be achieved; and only then would we begin to feel better about ourselves and our self-esteem needs would become met by feeling we have purpose.

Maslow believed that only when we had healthy self-esteem could we  move on to feeling self-fulfilled by achieving our full potential.

This makes so much sense when we are aiming to reach a state of happiness. Only by raising our levels of self-esteem  (respect for ourselves) can we become truly content.

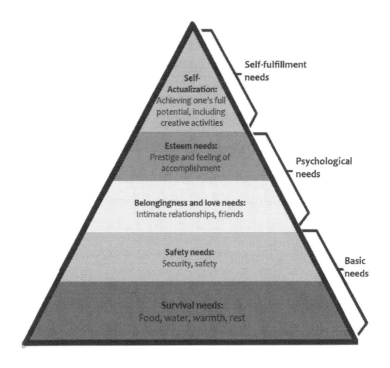

**Maslow's hierarchy of needs**

While I'm writing, Covid 19 has swept across the globe and everyday we hear of higher death tolls. People are advised to remain at least two metres apart from each other. We haven't seen members of our families for weeks, and many are losing jobs and loved ones because of the virus. Life has changed for everyone, beyond belief and quickly.

Everyone is experiencing it in different ways. Those with a secure base tend to be logical and are not worrying about an outcome they simply cannot predict. Those with an insecure base are struggling. Generally they are the ones thinking of an assortment of dark scenarios from conspiracy theories to future global wipe-out, each thought manifesting into another negative feeling. Fear is abundant and anxiety and depression are on the rise. It's no surprise that the sale of food and alcohol has increased as people find ways to soothe and comfort themselves (Scaffolding).

Many people's basic needs have been threatened. Many well-adjusted grown-ups are now feeling an insecurity they haven't experienced since childhood. The negative thinkers are constantly ruminating about an unknown future creating mass anxiety. Meanwhile, global pollution has fallen, wildlife is abundant, wartime-like camaraderie is prevalent and supermarkets are making a fortune.

**For every pile of poop there is a pile of gold. The one you wish to focus on is entirely up to you.**

## Questions:

It may be helpful to draw a timeline of your life, from birth to now, and write down any major milestones such as achievements, traumas, special events, relationships, education, employment etc. This will give you a clear overview of your life so far.

### How is your grown-up life?

1. Who are you in the Traffic Jam?

2. Do you feel secure or insecure within close relationships?

3. When have you experienced feeling vulnerable?

4. In what ways are you independent?

5. How capable do you feel about dealing with life?

6. How do you feel when you think about your past? (e.g. Peaceful, depressed).

7. How do you feel when you think about your future? (e.g. Excited, anxious).

8. Do you let people take advantage of you or do you take advantage of other people?

9. Do you achieve for yourself or for other people?

10. Do you feel you are equal to others and that you can do things at least as well as others?

# I DON'T FEEL OKAY
# YOUR SCAFFOLDING

When the Tower wobbles or cracks, your Scaffolding is never far away. Just like with young children and teenagers, adults have their Scaffolding of choice at hand. The list of avoidant and controlling behaviours is extensive. The Scaffolding is all designed to help you feel buoyant initially and then it becomes unsustainable and you don't feel so good.

Take gambling. The thrill of possibly winning fills you with excitement and hope and feel-good chemicals such as dopamine. This good feeling helps you avoid any uncomfortable feelings. You may win and experience high levels of dopamine, and therefore be likely to repeat the exercise to experience those feelings again. Eventually you will lose, and lose again, and again, but your body may be craving that dopamine hit so you continue to gamble. Soon the addiction causes problems in your financial as well as your personal life.

It is a similar scenario for those who take 'recreational' drugs in order to feel better. The first time they use the drug it produces a strong dopamine hit which feels really good. They take it again and again using higher doses, but repeatedly fail to attain that initial high. The user may experience uncomfortable emotions such as depression or guilt after the drug has worn off and may eventually suffer poor health and financial and/or personal problems.

Eating disorders help people feel in control initially. There is a certain satisfaction and pride in the numbers going down on the scales. However, deceit and then poor health are the long term price. Binge-eating brings about instant comfort, followed by feelings of guilt and disgust.

Over-working and over-exercising may keep uncomfortable thoughts and feelings at bay, but in the long term they often damage relationships and your own mental health.

Habitual personality traits also fall into the Scaffolding category. One such trait is People Pleasing.

As mentioned previously, a People Pleaser learned as a child that they could control their environment and feel better if they did good things for other people. This coping strategy may have served them well as children but they continued to use it and subconsciously embellished it through to adulthood.

Unfortunately, like with all Scaffolding, the feel-good benefits are only temporary.

The issue is that the People Pleaser truly believes that what *they* think is good for someone else is actually what that person wants or needs. They do not appreciate that the receiver may not want or need what the People Pleaser is giving them.

The People Pleaser will do things or give things to others regardless of whether others want them to or not. The People Pleaser believes that their behaviour and motives are coming from a good place (often heart-felt) and therefore this is what is best for the other person.

Many years ago I was at an elderly woman's home and noticed piles of old food packets, half-eaten jars of jam and other fetid groceries on her kitchen work surface. I decided to throw out all those items that looked beyond edible due to their sell-by-date or the presence of mould.

I certainly was feeling good about saving this woman from stomach complaints and I believed she'd be thrilled that I'd tidied up her kitchen for her.

I was fairly shocked and upset when she ushered me from her home and told me I had over-stepped the mark. It turned out that the woman used 'hoarding' as a way to feel safe and secure (her Scaffolding) and she was none too pleased with my interference. Thinking I was acting in her best interests I had behaved in a manner equal to throwing her treasured pet in the wheelie bin.

The People Pleaser often remains convinced they are right in their behaviour. It will rarely occur to them that they are being controlling by way of their 'I know what's best for you' attitude. They give in order to require the receiver to be grateful for what they have done for them. This causes them to feel good.

However, the person on the receiving end does not always feel grateful. Sometimes they don't want to be told what's best for them. In fact they feel belittled and looked down upon. The People Pleaser's behaviour can cause them to feel disempowered and even incapable (like the over-protective parent).

The People Pleaser ends up feeling hurt or resentful for giving and not being appreciated, but feels compelled to keep repeating the same behaviour in the hope of getting a different result (similar to the gambler and the drug user).

From a different perspective, if you are on the receiving end of someone who is always self-sacrificing it might be attractive to begin with and come across as loving and kind. After a while it may become difficult. You may be given things you don't really want or the person may be missing out themselves to put you before them which may cause you to feel guilty. They may always be doing things before you get a chance to, so you become dependent on them and start to lose your own sense of self and confidence.

Notice that when people escape from a controlling relationship they often say that their partner was wonderful to begin with, always doing things for them and making them feel special, and yet this turns sour when the person on the receiving end feels disempowered and unable to stand up for their self.

If you are an insecure person, and you experience this behaviour, you may start to see the People Pleaser as needy and controlling. If you are a more secure person you may start to wonder where the People Pleaser's self-respect is because no self-respecting person would keep giving of their self while resenting others for not being grateful.

Rather than the People Pleaser feeling better because of their behaviour, they end up feeling resentful and unappreciated.

This behaviour, like many forms of Scaffolding, only serves to lower self-esteem once it loses its feel-good factor.

You can now see that by taking responsibility for other people's feelings you were effectively telling them that you knew what was best for them and that they were not as capable as you. Now you realise that you are equal to others and you respect them as much as you respect yourself.

(We choose many activities for pleasure and they're not all Scaffolding. A Scaffolding activity is something that we do to avoid or control uncomfortable feelings. Usually different uneasy feelings will result as an after-effect of the activity. If we do something purely because it is pleasurable it is not Scaffolding and does not result in uncomfortable feelings, such as guilt or self-loathing.)

So, what is it that causes us not to feel okay as adults, and in turn causes us to turn to Scaffolding to shore us up?

As grown-ups we are in charge of our own lives and we can choose what we want to do, where we want to go, and who we want to be with.

The problem is that despite this we are following a Blueprint designed by someone else. This means that we are doing what we *should* do; we're going where we *ought* to go and we're in relationships with people who reflect what was familiar to us in our parents.

**Should, must and ought versus want, need and desire**

Externally we may have everything we need and yet internally we may be feeling unsettled, unhappy, overwhelmed or not good enough.

Sometimes we follow that part of our self that says we *should, ought* or *must* act or be a certain way.

We achieve this and emotionally we feel unfulfilled. Sometimes we follow our feeling-self that says we *want*, *need* or *desire*, and yet we are dissatisfied with the way life is turning out.

There are a few things going on here.

1. We are subconsciously following the Blueprint so, although we think we are making our own decisions about our job or housing etc, we are in fact tailoring our choices in line with our conditioning. This means that we end up doing what we believe we *should* do rather than what we *want* to do.

2. It is a confusing fact of life that we are attracted to and by people who are familiar to us (hence the word family). It's down to biology and reproduction, but we are more likely to be attracted to people with similar traits to our parents (which just sounds so wrong). Great news if yours are secure, assertive, kind and loving, not so great if yours are insecure alcoholics.

3. The majority of our thinking, feeling and behaviour is subconscious (as explained by the Iceberg) and if we experienced a high level of drama or trauma in our childhood and have insecure

parents our present and future will be experienced through the understanding and perspective we have gained through those events.

Now that we have this awareness, we are able to live more consciously and learn how to become more logical and rational. When we are ruled by logic there is often a more peaceful feeling within.

If you wanted to learn how a car worked you'd probably pop open the bonnet and someone would explain the different parts - engine, radiator, gearbox etc. When you're trying to understand why you don't feel okay, it's a good idea to know your different parts.

## Parent, Adult and Child parts

Psychiatrist Eric Berne the creator of Transactional Analysis (I'm okay, you're okay') explained these psychological parts.

In TA we are described as being made up of three main component parts – Parent, Adult and Child. Notice they are written with capitals so that they are not confused with you actually being a parent, an adult or a child.

Your Parent part is made up of the thoughts, feelings and behaviours that you have acquired, copied or learned from your parents.

This part can be controlling, protective and disempowering. This is where the *shoulds, musts* and *oughts* are. I think it, so it must be so.

There are two main elements to the Parent part. Critical Parent, which can be protective and disparaging, and Nurturing Parent, which can be caring and disempowering.

Your Adult part is your thoughts, feelings and behaviours based on all the experience and knowledge you've acquired until now.

It operates in the here and now and enables you to work things out in a logical, factual way. It is a fact, so it must be so. This part is rational and will challenge the reality of thoughts and feeling-states.

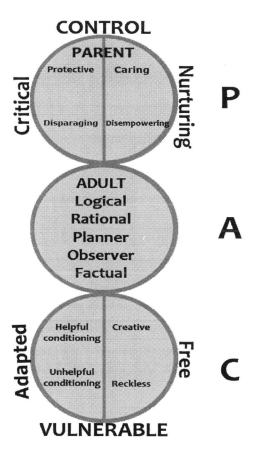

**Parent, Adult and Child parts**

Your Child part is your thoughts, feelings and behaviours being replayed from your childhood.

This part is emotional and makes decisions based on emotions. I feel it, therefore it must be so. This part can be fearful and restricted or reckless and free. This is where the *wants, needs* and *desires* are.

There are also two main Child parts. The Adapted child, which can have both helpful and unhelpful conditioning, and Free child, which can be both reckless and creative.

Whether you are 5 or 50 you will have these three parts. This is because a 5-year-old child can experience Adult (logical thinking) and Parent (controlling thinking in a critical way or a nurturing way), and a 50-year-old childless adult can display the Critical and Nurturing Parent part (when they look after someone else) as well as the Adapted and Free Child part, for example, if they are people-pleasing or playfully kicking Autumn leaves.

How did your parents interact with you? Depending on their mood at any given time they may have reacted differently. You may have dropped a drink on the carpet and you may have heard: "Oh dear, never mind, I'll get a cloth and clear it up" (Nurturing Parent). Or you may have heard: "You idiot, what do you think you are playing at? That carpet cost a fortune" (Critical Parent).

Most of us heard a mixture of the two and both parts have pros and cons. The Nurturing Parent can sometimes be disempowering by way of their 'rescuing' techniques, and Critical Parent can help a person feel secure and protected.

In essence, the Parent part comprises of the internalised messages we received from our parents as we grew up. Its purpose is to control us with *shoulds, musts,* and *oughts*. You *should* clean your teeth; you *must* go to school and you *ought* to eat healthily.

The reason for the control is to keep the Child part safe and healthy, because the Child part *wants, needs* and *desires*. The Child part is driven by emotions. These are the emotions that we learned as young children.

Sometimes a person may appear to over-react to a situation. Their emotional outburst may appear to be out of proportion with the event. This is probably because, as a child, they were particularly affected by an event, such as witnessing their parents fighting.

Later in life they see two people fighting and the event subconsciously reminds them of (or triggers) memories of the way they felt as a child. They might then appear to be overly frightened in response to this latter event.

Critical Parent may communicate to your vulnerable Child part that you shouldn't change or the Nurturing Parent part may tell you that you mustn't change. Your Child part listens to these controlling parts and is scared to change or believes it would be incapable of it.

The Adult part is mainly what we learn by experience and education. This part is logical, rational and factual. Its function is to create a reasonable balance between the Parent and Child parts.

Generally, the Parent part assumes a  powerful 'one up' position of 'I'm okay, you're not okay', whereas the vulnerable Child part is more often 'You're okay, I'm not okay'. The balanced Adult part is 'I'm okay, you're okay'.

Someone with an insecure Foundation and therefore lower self-esteem, is more likely to have a higher percentage of  the adverse Parent and Child parts (disparaging, disempowering, unhelpful conditioning and reckless traits).

Those with a secure Foundation and healthy self-esteem are more likely to have a higher percentage of the favourable Parent and Child parts (protective, caring, helpful conditioning and creative traits). The Adult part tends to be the biggest part in secure people and the smallest part in insecure people.

Let's look at a scenario involving an insecure, passive person. She texts a friend and they haven't replied. Three days have gone by.

Her adverse Parent part says (as an inner voice): "Well, nobody likes someone who is so needy. You should be less needy. You really ought to say sorry and make the peace."

The Child part feels sad, lonely, rejected and not good enough. The adverse Child part says: "I knew they didn't like me. I'm just not a nice person, no wonder they haven't texted me back."

**Child, Adult and Parent Inner Dialogue**

Your Adult part may or may not step in here. Sometimes the Parent and Child parts are so loud that the Adult just sits quietly in the background. If the Adult can be heard, it is likely to say: "Just hang on a minute you two. Maybe our friend never received the text. Maybe they meant to reply and simply forgot. When we last saw them they did not behave as if they didn't like us. If we haven't heard back by the weekend we'll call again."

It's the Adult part which is likely to be pro-active and perhaps phone the friend and ensure they have received the message. This in turn appeases the Child part and quietens the Parent part. It's no wonder we sometimes don't feel okay!

When you begin to explore your Foundation you will be able to assess whether you are more secure and assertive or insecure; whether you are more passive or aggressive; whether you are have more positive or negative internalised Parent and Child parts, and how strong and loud your Adult part is.

As a grown-up, these three parts are at their prime and will be simultaneously working alongside your Wiring, Windows and Blueprint. You have become a finely untuned machine. You have a perfectly imperfect Smart Brain.

Using the Parent, Adult and Child parts we can look at another diagram and TA theory which explains further why we sometimes feel in a pickle.

## The Drama Triangle

The Drama Triangle is another way of looking at how we socially interact and why our Brickwork cracks and crumbles when there is an insecure Foundation. TA teacher Stephen Karpman created the triangle to illustrate the various roles we play in life.

He explains that we all have a familiar starting position – Persecutor, Rescuer or Victim – and from that role we switch from one role to another depending on the roles played by others. It's like we do a strange triangular dance with the people we interact with.

The roles of Persecutor and Rescuer are 'Parent' type roles and are therefore controlling. The role of Victim is a 'Child' type role and so portrays as vulnerable. Adult is logical, factual and rational.

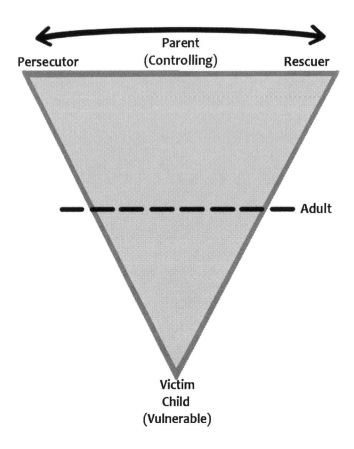

**The Drama Triangle**

When we have been brought up in a household where love is conditional: "I'll show you love when you behave how I want and withdraw it when you don't," you are likely to move to the Victim position when you are told off; to Persecutor when you become angry at being told off; and then to Rescuer if you then apologise for being angry or for getting it wrong to start with.

Meanwhile, the person who told you off, the Persecutor, moves to Victim when you become angry with them and then they may return to Persecutor or Rescuer themselves in order to control the conflict if you do not apologise.

You may notice that again the titles Persecutor, Rescuer and Victim have capitals, and that is because these roles reflect the Parent and Child parts. Persecutor is adverse Critical Parent part, Rescuer is adverse Nurturing Parent part, and Victim is the adverse Child part.

Persecutor and Rescuer, just like the Parent part, are there to gain control. The Victim feels like it is vulnerable and lacking power like Child.

Many of us grew up in environments where the Drama Triangle was being played out in front of and around us. We were being drawn into it, without any awareness of this happening, certainly by us and probably by the people around us. The Drama Triangle was part of our Foundation and became part of our Framework (or conditioned-self), and we learned how to move between the roles while those around us did the same.

There is also a fourth role and this is one we were less likely to witness very often if we had insecure parents. This is the role of Adult. Adult is not to be confused with being a grown-up.

Just like in the Parent, Adult and Child parts, Adult here represents the logical, rational and factual side of you. It is not led by emotion as with the Child part and is not led by control as with the Parent part.

In the Drama Triangle if you play the roles of Persecutor, Rescuer or Victim you are in the game of drama. When you take up the role of Adult you cease to play. You are out of the game. You are no longer in the drama. In Adult the world feels more peaceful and less......... well, dramatic.

We'll look more into how to move into Adult later, but this chapter is looking at reasons why we feel uncomfortable or not okay in ourselves.

By living and growing up within the Drama Triangle it is likely that you will be conditioned into spending more time in certain roles, depending on the roles of your parents.

Earlier, we looked at the People Pleaser. This may have been someone who grew up in a hostile environment, perhaps like an aggressive dad hitting a passive mum (or maybe much more subtle than that), and the child believing she could somehow control the situation by being good or by trying to please her parents.

(Interestingly, the People Pleaser adapted their behaviour when they were a child to feel safer in the drama they lived in. They were effectively victims of their environment; they tried to rescue their parents by being good or pleasing them, and might inwardly persecute themselves for getting it wrong if they were unable to control their parents' behaviours.)

If we freeze-frame the above scenario, mum might play the Victim, dad the Persecutor and their child would be the Rescuer. When the child grows up, due to her Foundation and Framework she may become an insecure, passive-aggressive, People Pleaser. She has a predisposition to play the role of Rescuer.

Let's think of her now as a wife and mother herself, and look at the drama that may unfold in her household as she and her children wait for dad to return home.

Dad's starting position is Persecutor because of course she chose a partner with familiar traits to her own father. He is returning from work and is expected at 5.30pm. Mum, in her starting position of Rescuer, wants the household atmosphere to be calm when he gets home, in an attempt to minimise any conflict.

She knows that if the children are not quiet and dinner isn't on the table when dad gets home, the household is going to be subjected to a hostile atmosphere due to dad's predisposition.

As he enters the house mum is beginning to feel that old familiar fear as she thinks: "Have I done enough to control his temper?" She is now moving into the position of Victim and her children are feeling this Victim state also due to their conditioning. Mum took up the role of Persecutor to ensure the children complied with her attempts to pacify dad.

Although all the children are brought up in the same household and conditioned in the same way, their starting positions could be any of the three roles, depending on their own individual Blueprints. Just because they have the same Groundwork, Foundation and Framework does not mean that their Wiring and Windows will be the same as their siblings. Their Smart Brains may have interpreted the same events in different ways.

Dad begins to eat his dinner and makes a remark about the food, that mum, with her particular set of Windows, perceives as critical. She hears that he is not grateful and quickly goes from Victim to Persecutor, because she feels hurt and then resentful. Dad didn't mean his remark to be taken so personally and therefore didn't realise he'd been placed in the position of Persecutor. He can't understand why mum is being off with him. He goes from confused Victim to Rescuer and resolves this particular drama by telling mum that the dinner is lovely and he was only joking about hard potatoes.

All is well again for a short time.

Drama is exhausting.

By looking at this type of scenario we can see why some people's lives feel so up and down and insecure.

They are continually trying to second-guess the needs of others and then feeling powerless and resentful when their behaviour is not controlling the world around them. They feel out-of-control and overwhelmed.

We go around these triangles and cycles time and again, and use more avoidant and controlling methods in an attempt to ease the inner turmoil and pain.

At some point we realise we want to stop. We want to stop repeating the same patterns, we want to stop feeling bad about ourselves. We want to stop our avoidant and controlling behaviours because they just cause us to feel worse eventually.

You are not a child any more and as an Adult you have a right to do and say what you feel is right. By asserting yourself in this way you are showing others that you expect respect.

**Falling down the same holes**

As mentioned before, sometimes life feels like we are continually falling down the same holes. We walk down the same well-trodden path and fall down a hole. The next day we walk down the path and fall down the same hole. This goes on for years and we are totally unaware of the holes and our crash landings.

Somewhere in our subconscious we know we hurt and need something to soothe our pain. We turn to coping methods and find ways to avoid the pain or control the pain. Sometimes the holes represent the way we think about ourselves or the world around us; sometimes the holes represent our familiar feelings; sometimes the holes represent our habitual behaviours and sometimes the holes represent our repeat ways of coping.

When you work on yourself you begin to develop self-awareness. You then start to become aware that the holes represent your inner conflict created by your Foundation and Framework. The *shoulds, oughts* and *musts* versus your *wants*, *needs* and *desires*. At this point, you metaphorically walk down the path, you see the holes and then you fall down them.

Consciously you become aware of the holes and you are aware of your methods of coping with them. You think about your Blueprint and think there is nothing you can do about that, so you decide to do what you can.

You may consciously decide to stop drinking, stop gambling, lose weight, gain weight and so on. Of course you are able to do all these things for a limited period of time. The reason you can do this is because you are in fact, taking control by using willpower and determination and this feels good. This control is likely to be another coping method (a piece of Scaffolding).

As with all Scaffolding, this control eventually ceases. We are not able to sustain it because our Blueprint hasn't changed, and so we revert to type (like a memory-foam pillow) and find ourselves back in the cycle.

**Questions:**

**What holes do you repeatedly fall down?**

1. Do you have a habit of negative thinking?

2. How do you put yourself down?

3. Do you moan about life and people?

4. Do you expect to be unlucky and for things to go wrong?

5. Do you often feel low for no reason?

6. How do you feel before reaching for Scaffolding?

7. What do you do to feel better?

8. What are your Parent, Adult and Child parts like?

9. In what ways do you recognise the Drama Triangle?

10. How does your Scaffolding impact on yourself and others?

# WHAT PREVENTS CHANGE?
# YOUR SNAGGING

When you discover what is keeping you in this holding pattern of repeat behaviours sustainable changes can begin to take place.

You have looked at what causes your Tower to wobble and what measures you  take by way of Scaffolding to keep it from falling. You know that these measures are temporary and what you'd really like is long term change. So what stops you?

Many of my clients come to counselling because they want to stop the Scaffolding. They focus on their over-eating or under-eating, their drug use, their relationship issues, their gambling habits, and think that by addressing them, they will feel content.

**Leaves on a tree**

I ask them to imagine their various vices and coping methods as leaves on a tree (rather than Scaffolding around their Tower). The leaves represent anything they may do in order to avoid or control their emotional turmoil. As previously discussed the list of choices is vast.

I then ask them to look at the trunk of the tree to discover what is happening in their life right now that cause the leaves to grow. This could be anything from not liking their job, their relationship, and most often, not liking themselves.

We then look at the root of the tree to explore what messages they received in childhood that caused that trunk to develop. Once we deal with the root, the leaves simply fall off the tree.

If we just focused on eliminating the leaves two things would happen. Firstly, because we were focusing on what we don't want, we will surely increase this behaviour (as explained later) and secondly, if we could succeed in ridding someone of the leaves (or Scaffolding), new and sometimes different leaves would grow or their Tower would collapse. Not good results.

**Leaves on a tree**

## Underpinning

Instead, we focus on Underpinning, because this is the project that strengthens the Foundation. This is what makes improvements to the base on which everything else stands. Underpinning is developing self-esteem, assertiveness and a strong Adult part. This is when we can honestly think and feel 'I'm okay and you're okay'.

When this work is done the Scaffolding will fall away bit by bit on its own (just like the leaves).

You can't change what was put into your Foundation or the creation of your Blueprint, but you can add more quality materials to make your Tower structurally sound and this subtly alters your Blueprint.

When you Underpin your Foundation (learn assertiveness in order to develop healthy self-esteem) you begin to change your Blueprint from insecure to secure. Simultaneously your Tower will effectively be Re-Wired and have new Windows installed (healthy self-esteem helps to improve your logical thinking and gives you a more realistic perspective). Your Tower will feel more secure and therefore will require less Scaffolding.

First, let's explore your Snagging.

Your Snagging is what prevented you from sticking to that diet, climbing that career ladder, or quitting smoking. It is the reason why you can see the holes and yet still feel compelled to fall down them. If your Foundation and Framework created the holes it was also your Foundation and Framework that created the fears and habits that compel you to fall down them.

**Fear and habits**

Your conditioning made sure of two things: a) fear would cause you to behave in certain ways and continue to behave like this, and b) habit ensured continued use of these behaviours by way of repetition.

Your parents wanted you to behave in a way that conformed with their expectations. If you didn't you may have been punished, even if that was by a look or changed tone of voice. You learned to avoid that uncomfortable feeling of 'getting it wrong' by doing what was required. You adapted.

You also subconsciously watched your parents and learned their ways of thinking, feeling and behaving by mimicking them and repeating their reactions until you formed habits.

Any feelings of fear that created a habit then, is the same fear that has kept you trapped in that habit today.

Fear and habit are the two most powerful driving forces that keep you where you are. Fear of change manifests in various ways, such as: "What if I stop doing what I do or being who I am? People might not like me or I might not like myself." Your subconscious fears that your life may change and it may not be for the better.

Your subconscious only wants to keep you alive and: "You are alive right now, so let's not change anything," is its command to your Smart Brain.

A man I met, who was HIV positive, asked me for a healing session as I was a Reiki practitioner.

During the treatment, although he was laying seemingly relaxed and not moving on my therapy couch, I sensed that he did not want to be healed.

After the session I asked him why he didn't want the healing he had requested. He began to cry and replied that if he wasn't HIV positive he wouldn't know who he was.

Being HIV positive had provided him with support, doctors, hospital appointments and the routine of medication. He feared that to be free of HIV would leave him feeling lost.

Consciously he wanted to be well yet subconsciously it felt too scary to change.

Habit is sustained by fear. To change a habit means facing the fear of what change might bring.

Habits we developed many years ago may no longer serve us well, but we continue to use them because of the fear of change.

Habits can become so automatic that we don't even realise we have them, such as the habit of negative thinking.

## Fear and negative thinking

If we go right back to when our ancestors were cavemen and cavewomen our biology ensured we were more likely to think negatively than positively. This was crucial for the survival of the Human Race.

If a caveman was skipping joyfully through the forests thinking: "What a wonderful sunny day," feeling at ease and happy, and his body was producing lovely feel-good hormones, he might very quickly be eaten up by a Sabre-toothed tiger.

So, our Smart Brains were programmed to think about what bad things might happen and to feel the fear that that thought creates. In that way the cavemen would be vigilant to incoming carnivores. He would be thinking about a tiger jumping him, he would feel afraid, and his body would produce stress hormones such as cortisol and adrenaline, ready for fighting. As a result of this line of thinking he lives to see another day.

If you think back to your childhood, it may be no surprise that you remember the negative things, like being told off for not eating your sprouts, 'cold shouldered' for using bad language, or smacked for stealing, rather than the positives. We tend to remember bad feelings in order to avoid them in the future.

Do you remember being praised for tidying your bedroom, being given a reward for being kind, getting a pat on the back for passing a spelling test or being cheered-on during sports day?

Your subconscious is programmed to keep you alive and that is why you are more likely to remember negatives rather than positives.

When you feel happy, content, peaceful and at ease you are not motivated in any way to do anything other than what you are doing. When you feel sad, angry, upset or afraid you definitely feel like you need to do something to change these feelings. That is why people come to counselling when they feel negative rather than when they are happy.

What all this means is that you are likely to experience negative feelings when you start to think of what you *should, ought* or *must* do. In other words, what you were conditioned to believe you *should, ought* or *must* do, rather than what you *want* to do.

Let's take work as an example. You were possibly conditioned that you *should* go to work when you grow up or you are lazy. It's what your parents expected of you perhaps. You then internalised their expectation and created a belief about yourself that you *should* go to work. As a grown-up, you may feel guilty if you do not have a job or are not constantly busy working.

In this example, fearing the feeling of guilt will generally motivate you to work, therefore ensuring you conform with your conditioning, or you may choose not to work and therefore have to use Scaffolding to cope with the uncomfortable feelings of guilt created by what you *should* do versus what you *want* to do.

As you are also governed by the pleasure and pain discipline, you may take either the route of work, get paid and don't feel guilt, or don't work, get benefits, and drink. Whichever you choose may then be the one you repeat until it becomes a habit.

After a while the worker-you may dream of staying home drinking, but fears not having a regular income and feeling guilty; and the you-at-home fears going to work and being incapable of whatever is asked of you due to loss of confidence.

## The problems of habit

You quickly learned to behave in ways that were expected of you. You then continued to repeat these behaviours to avoid fear and because of habit. The behaviours became habitual subconscious actions rather than considered responses.

We use conscious responses to learn to drive, read, write, play the piano or ride a bicycle. All these activities start as considered actions and at some point they become so familiar to us that we no longer have to think how to do them. We do them automatically and they become subconscious reactions.

Have you ever tried to unlearn how to write or try to forget how to drive a car? It's really hard.

## The Tea Towel Analogy

This illustrates why habits are so difficult to change. You, like most of us, may have a tea towel hanging in your kitchen. Maybe that tea towel hangs in the same place all the time. You hang it there because it is convenient and easy to reach when you need to use it. You don't have to stop and consider where it is, you can go straight to it.

Now let's swap that tea towel for a habit you have. It may be an external habit such as smoking or eating when you are bored or it might be an internal habit like getting angry in a traffic jam or being a People Pleaser.

Now that you have acknowledged the habit, you may even be able to acknowledge what fearful feelings manifest if you imagine giving it up, such as: "I will be grumpy if I stop smoking. I'll have to face being productive if I eat less. I don't know who will get my anger if not the traffic. People might not like me if I don't people please."

You are reading this book because there are aspects of your life or your self that you are not content with. You are fed up with the metaphorical tea towel hanging where it is and have decided to move it.

In the Tea Towel Analogy you move it to a new place in the kitchen. This makes so much more sense, a far better place for it. What happens when you automatically (subconsciously) go to reach for the tea towel? You go straight back to the old habitual place on autopilot.

At this point you may decide to put it back where it was, or you may use willpower and perseverance to establish the new habit of reaching for the tea towel where it now hangs.

In this scenario you have actually removed the tea towel from its old place, and the empty space reminds you to go to the new place. After a while you form a new habit.

Because the tea towel has actually moved you soon begin to learn consciously and then subconsciously that it is in a new place and after only a short while of practising you find yourself automatically going to the new place on autopilot.

However, with real habits they are still there, cigarettes are still for sale, the anger is still within you, the self-sabotage and procrastination and the need to people please are still there.

Because no one has actually removed your habit it is much more difficult to break. Add to this the fear of not having the habit and you begin to see what you're up against.

Imagine, that by moving the metaphorical tea towel, feelings of anxiety and guilt begin to surface.

What if you move the tea towel to a preferred place and someone else keeps moving it back to its original spot. Not only are you competing with your own internal underminer who is subconsciously trying to get you to return it to its former hanging place (because that is Smart Brain efficiency), but now someone else prefers it where it was and so is externally undermining your successful change of habit. Then they top this by criticising your attempts to change and so you experience negative feelings such as more guilt or humiliation.

**The Underminers**

As we can see, internal and external underminers will try to sabotage your success and reinforce your habit.

Let's look at a weight issue. You want to lose a stone so you join a gym or a slimming club. You have hung your tea towel in a new place. However, as you have not addressed the negative emotions that hold you at a stone heavier (fear, habit and false beliefs) you may as well cancel the gym membership and hang your tea towel back where it was.

While you have subconscious fears and habits and hold the belief that you are fat, you will revert to form.

Let's assume you have great willpower and perseverance, and you stick with your plan and lose a stone. Your own underminer convinces you that you are still fat  so you eat to comfort yourself (you return the tea towel to its original place). Or your partner (you are likely to be attracted to what is familiar) verbally puts you down in order to sabotage your success and healthier looks because they now feel inadequate and insecure (they return the tea towel). When you try to move the tea towel to its new place your partner says something which causes you to feel negative so you conform to their conditions (your Foundation and Framework is still being reinforced).

You have several choices here. Leave your partner, forget the weight loss, or learn assertiveness and grow healthy self-esteem in order to get your needs met without trampling over others or being trampled over by others.

You can easily get your needs met without violating the rights of others and that is why you have decided to stand up for yourself from this day forward.

You recognise that by respecting yourself you are training others to respect you and by showing them respect you are treating them as you demand to be treated. You expect respect and respect others in return.

## I feel it so strongly, it must be true

Have you ever felt so in love that you took it for granted that your partner felt the same way about you? It might be true that you felt so loved because you were so loved or it may not be true.

Have you ever felt so angry that you were convinced someone had wronged you? Maybe they had, or maybe you thought they had and this led to your intense feeling. Maybe they hadn't wronged you and it was only your perception (due to your Windows).

This intense feeling that the thought created, then feeds back into your thoughts, and you are convinced they have wronged you, otherwise why would you feel so angry.

Back to The Traffic Jam. Is it the traffic jam that causes someone's anger or the person's internal aggressive filter that causes them to think angry thoughts and these cause them to experience angry feelings?

How about this one? You think your hair looks a mess today so as you walk down the road you are feeling self-conscious about your hair. Every time you pass someone you think: "I bet they are looking at how bad my hair  is." You feel more self-conscious and keep your head down or pull your hood up.

You think it's a mess and therefore you feel uncomfortable. Maybe you feel embarrassment so strongly that you are certain they must be laughing at you.

Our emotional feelings are nothing more than a reflection of our thinking. Our thinking is the meaning we place on an event based on our internal Wiring and Windows. If we think it is true, we feel it is true. What if what we think is not true?

What if we didn't think the thought to start with?

What if you left the house without looking in the mirror and you didn't see that your hair was in a mess. You walk down the road smiling at everyone you pass. You feel sociable and happy, and everyone you pass has a big ol' grin on their face. You feel confident and happy that everyone is truly pleased to see you today. You think to yourself: "They look so pleased to see me," so you feel happy, confident and sociable.

If the glass in your Windows was distorted by your Foundation and Framework, it is likely that this distortion will ensure you think about things in a negative way and therefore feel negative about yourself and your surroundings. This habitual reaction will keep you where you have always been, within your Blueprint.

Maybe you can now see how 'I feel it so strongly, it must be true' can give you inaccurate views. It can also be said: "I think, therefore I am," and we can see why that could be true. Shakespeare once wrote: "There is nothing either good or bad, but thinking makes it so."

Let's try another exercise. Think of a holiday or another experience you really enjoyed. Take your imagination back to that time and picture it in your minds' eye. See what you see, notice the colours and any movement in the image. Listen for any sounds, notice any smells, maybe you can almost reach out and touch aspects of the scene. Now become aware of how you are feeling emotionally. Are you relaxed, calm, happy, content, excited, or some other positive feeling?

Now let's do the same exercise with a situation that did not go so well for you. Think about that time now. Play it out in your mind's eye almost as if it was playing on a video. See what you see. Notice if the colours are as bright in this memory. Hear what you hear, smell what you smell, taste what you taste, and feel how it feels to have this memory. Not very pleasant?

When you think about something you create an image in your mind. Many people create visual images in their mind's eye, but for some the images use other senses such as hearing or feeling. When you think a thought and you create an image, the corresponding feelings will manifest within you. Your physical body is tricked into believing the event is actually taking place, and corresponding happy or stress chemicals will be released into your system accordingly.

Dreams work in the same way. How often have you woken up from a sexy dream and felt amorous, woken from a nightmare and felt afraid, or woken from a  happy dream and tried to get back to sleep to continue feeling happy?

In a dream, your mind creates pictures and stories based on your unconscious thoughts; your body feels the related emotions and your body releases the corresponding hormones.

This means you have the power to release feel-good chemicals into your body by creating positive thoughts, images and feelings without even getting out of bed!

Of course, that also means that you have the power to release  more harmful chemicals, such as cortisol into your system without anything bad actually happening to you, just by the way you think.

When you become conscious of your thought processes, your feeling-state becomes your choice.

This is very important information because knowing this can help you to experience better feeling-states. If your conditioning leads you to think negatively, then your habit of thinking the worst will truly ensure that you spend a lot of time feeling discomfort.

## Think the worst and constantly feel anxious

If you suffer from the habit (or over-use) of negative thinking you may be able to relate to the following situation and how I experienced it.

I learned the habit of imagining what was the worst that could happen in some misplaced expectation that if the worst actually did happen I would somehow be ready for it and it would impact me less. I lived my life in this constant state of fearing the worst happening and therefore not enjoying myself until such a time as the worst didn't happen.

I first learned how this did not serve me well on a counselling course. As I drove home from that course I remember thinking: "I bet when I get home the kids would have made themselves a meal and not cleared up. My partner will look at me in a disapproving way and I will feel like a bad mother and a bad girlfriend and I'll feel guilty and feel obligated to tell my kids off and then they will hate me." (This certainly speaks volumes about my former Wiring and Windows).

Needless to say I started to worry about going home. The more I thought these thoughts, the more anxious I felt and the more I dreaded going home.

I then remembered some learning earlier that day, and realised that whether I thought about the worst scenario or a better scenario, it would make no difference to the reality of what had actually been going on at home while I was out. So I chose to imagine that they had cleared up after themselves and the atmosphere was relaxed at home. I thoroughly enjoyed the rest of my journey home with this positive thought in mind.

I recognised that my thinking had no impact on the reality of what had actually happened. My thinking only had an impact on how I felt. Due to my change of thoughts my feeling-state changed from anxious to relaxed.

So when people say to me: "If I think that the worst will happen, anything better is a bonus," I tell them about my journey.

I tell them that I too believed that if I was always prepared for something bad to happen then when or if it did I would have cushioned the blow by being prepared. But, in reality this simply isn't true.

I am no more protected if something bad does happen and I'm possibly in a worse head-space to deal with it.

Just like with the caveman, it is helpful to *consider* anything bad that could happen so that you can take steps to minimise the chance of it taking place. However, the habit of over-using negative thinking can be debilitating whereas a quick risk assessment can be helpful.

The habit of over-using negative thoughts will certainly keep you in your old and familiar cycles.

Every day you notice yourself thinking more positively; experiencing more positive feelings and behaving in a calm and assertive way.

**False and limiting beliefs**

The beliefs you hold about yourself were programmed into you in childhood. That Metaphorical Mirror that your parents held up to you told you who you were and you believed it.

You used the Teflon and Velcro Effects (rejected or accepted information) to reinforce these beliefs about yourself and your place in the world ever since.

It's interesting that as teenagers we could challenge our parents about their views and beliefs about politics and roast dinners but we never challenged who they told us we were.

It never even crossed our minds to question what we were led to believe about ourselves.

Do you feel loveable, worthy and able to cope with whatever life throws at you or do you feel deficient, and afraid of what will happen next?

Once your Windows developed it was difficult to see things any differently.

This is why you can totally disagree with someone else who is looking at the same thing as you are.

As an example let's consider the scenario of twins who were adopted at birth. Genetics have made their mark and maybe even the first few days of their life have made an impact on who they believe they are, but they then go to live with two very different families.

Both families live in reasonable areas, with average schools and their incomes and work schedules are similar. The only real difference is the adoptive parents.

Child A lives with parents who are basically secure. They don't think they are particularly better or worse than others. They just feel okay with who they are. They are relaxed and take life as it comes. They feel loveable and capable of giving love. They feel worthy and respect themselves and their boundaries and those of others. If they need or want something they will simply ask for it and if it is unavailable to them they quickly learn to accept what is, is. Their filter is secure, assertive and Adult, and their Windows view reality without distortions.

Child B goes to parents who are insecure. Father's Windows (due to his Foundation) show him that the world is against him and everyone is out to get him. He is suspicious, angry, has aggressive outbursts and he is the angry man in The Traffic Jam. People always make him angry. Father is strict and critical and believes that if you do wrong you must be punished. He shouts a lot.

Mother is different in many ways, although still insecure. She is passive and views the world as a scary place in which she never feels safe. She worries a lot about everything. She thinks negatively and will always find a problem for every solution. She tends to be over-protective of her child and is constantly telling Child B to be careful; she does whatever she can for the child to avoid him getting it wrong or hurting himself.

Now you can really begin to see how these two opposite exaggerations can mould the children simply by them living in these two very different environments.

Both children, due to their genetics, inherit their former relatives' talents for numbers, and are  bright when it comes to mathematics.

They both take maths homework to their parents for help. Child A is only just learning how to add up and his parents are supportive, nurturing and patient. They allow him to have time with the sum, to mull it over without pressure and they find practical ways to demonstrate with counters or buttons how to solve the problems. When he gets the question correct they say: "Well done," and when he gets it wrong they say: "Well tried."

At Child B's house an identical situation occurs. However, as child B sits with his maths book open his father gives a different response.  He has little patience and begins to pressurise the child into answering the questions. The child feels intimidated and fears he will get it wrong and get shouted at. His mind fogs over. He can't think straight and he is sure he'll get the answer wrong. Actually despite it all he got the answer right, but by this time father was not focusing and mistakenly reads his son's answer incorrectly. He tells the boy he will never be any good at maths and looks at him in a disappointed and angry way.

Child A's filter (Windows) is already being created. "I feel okay and I'm pretty confident when it comes to maths." In the future if Child A gets a sum correct his Smart Brain accepts that information and it reinforces that he is good at maths.

The subconscious being what it is, will hang on to that correct sum like the Velcro Effect because it fits with its belief. When Child A gets a sum wrong he is patient with himself, asks for help and never lets the mistake define who he is (the Teflon Effect is activated). He knows he is okay and so are others.

As for Child B, every time he gets a sum right he thinks it must be some kind of fluke or a particularly easy sum because he has been told he is no good at maths. His subconscious has taken this message and uses every opportunity to reinforce it. When Child B gets a sum correct he brushes it away because it doesn't make sense to his Smart Brain and the Teflon Effect takes place. However whenever he gets a sum wrong or struggles to find the answer, his subconscious takes it as confirmation that he is indeed no good at maths (the Velcro Effect is activated).

These are just isolated situations, but imagine the reality of the continuous environments created by these two families, the learned behaviours and the strong conditioning the children are open to, every day for around 16 years. That's a lot of conditioning, moulding and brainwashing. The boys' abilities were basically identical but because of who their parents metaphorically told them they were, their Foundations and Frameworks were set and their Blueprints were written.

Child A had a healthy belief system and would likely grow to be confident, assertive, logical and rational.

Child B would likely have a distorted belief system. He may suffer low self-esteem and become either aggressive like father to get his needs met or passive like mother to avoid confrontation. He will probably believe he is not capable of dealing with what life throws his way and that he is not deserving of good things.

The truth is that both children were loveable, capable, bright and deserving, but one of them was shown a false image in that mirror and he believed without question what he was shown.

You believe in yourself, you know you are capable and deserving of happiness, and the respect you have for yourself will cause the Ripple Effect which ensures that others treat you with the respect you deserve also. Every day you feel happier and freer to live the life you wish to live.

**Self Sabotage and self punishment**

When you believe negative things about yourself you tend not to like yourself. When you don't like yourself you are unlikely to treat yourself well.

Subconsciously you do not believe you deserve good things, so when good things happen you unconsciously sabotage them. If you were conditioned with punishment you internalised this and continue to punish yourself, verbally or by the way you treat yourself, long after you leave home.

How many times have you set out to do something and not completed it? Maybe you consciously wanted to lose weight and your Adult self knew that all you had to do was exercise more and eat less. Yet, a lifetime of wanting this outcome and trying many times to achieve it has left you still falling short of your target. Why do some people work so hard to climb the career ladder and yet when they see their goal is within reach, something appears to come along and sabotage their achievement?

This is how the game of Snakes and Ladders plays out because a person consciously wants one thing (they climb up the ladder towards it) and yet is subconsciously being pulled back (they slide down a snake) to their familiar Foundation and Framework (because of the Teflon and Velcro Effects generated by their Smart Brain).

How about this one?

You meet the love of your life and yet feel desperately insecure that they are going to leave you. You actually have met the love of your life and they feel the same way about you.

However, your internal insecurity (which of course was put in place during your childhood) causes you to fret relentlessly about them leaving you and you continually ask them for reassurance and question where they've been and who they've been with. Eventually your partner is so exasperated with your constant interrogation and mistrust of them, that they do actually leave you. You, of course, can then say: "I told you so," and of course you would, because your subconscious will do everything in its power to reinforce your beliefs about yourself. This self-fulfilling prophecy means you are creating what you believe will happen to you.

When you subconsciously believe that you don't deserve what you desire you subconsciously sabotage your successes and then punish yourself for your failures.

Have you ever verbally beaten yourself up and spoken badly to yourself rather than treating yourself with compassion and kindness?

## Internal Dialogue

Most of us speak to ourselves. We have internal voices that hold an internal dialogue or narrative as our day-to-day life unfolds.

The way you talk to yourself is the direct result of your own unique inner Parent, Adult and Child commentary. How these parts interact with one another determines whether you are harsh and critical of yourself or kind and compassionate. This internal perspective is then reflected externally to give you your external view of the world.

Going back to that angry person in The Traffic Jam, can you begin to imagine how his internal dialogue plays out? It must be most uncomfortable carrying all that inner anger around. How about the anxious driver's dialogue about the boss sacking him. The turmoil they both feel internally, telling themselves how awful and scary the world is, must be exhausting. The secure and assertive driver turns off the engine, switches up the radio and enjoys the world being forced to slow down for a few minutes while they relax. Their inner narrative is likely to be calm, compassionate and rational.

It would make sense therefore that if the messages you received as a child were that you were not good enough, it was your fault or that you were unlovable, your inner dialogue would reflect this. The way you speak to yourself would correspond with your adapted Child part feeling inferior and blamed, so you'd hear Victim language such as: "It's all my fault, no one loves me," and your Parent part would reinforce this by using critical language.

Unfortunately it would be likely that your Adult voice would be too weak to communicate logic and rationale to these imposing parts.

In this example, if you made a mistake, your internal dialogue may go something like: "Oh, great, you just can't ever get it right can you? (Parent) I'm so useless. I always get it wrong. I'm so stupid.

(Child) Yep, you certainly are stupid. Other people manage to get it right. You are stupid (Parent)." And so it goes on throughout every day of your life, reinforcing those early messages.

We then go on to tell other people how stupid we are: "You won't believe what a stupid thing I did today," and this further reinforces our beliefs and internal voices.

By speaking to yourself in this way you are repeatedly punishing yourself by telling yourself how stupid you are. Ironically, you then feel bad and need something to help you feel better. Of course, you turn to your Scaffolding and then you can later berate yourself about that too.

You are already more assertive and confident than before and this is why people are now treating you with more respect. Every day you are becoming more assertive and your belief in yourself and your own abilities grows stronger. Every day you tell yourself "I am capable. I am deserving" and you find life is calmer and you feel happier.

**Direction**

When I ask clients how they would like their lives to look, how would they like to feel or where they see themselves five years from now, I am often answered with a list of things they don't like about their lives and themselves and they have little idea what they do want.

At best, they may say: "I want to be happy," but they do not know what they need to create that happiness. This is a bit like going to a bus station and walking up to the ticket office and saying: "I don't know where I want to go, but I want to be happy when I get there." When you don't know what you do want or where you do want to go, you simply drift through life without purpose.

When you decide what you would like, then the possible routes to get there will open up for you.

Some people like to drift through life without setting themselves any goals or destinations, and that may be okay for them. But how would it be to really live your life on purpose? Actually deciding what you would like from it and getting there?

I wonder how you would like your life to look five years from now?

**The memory-foam pillow**

Negative thoughts, feelings, habits, conditioning, expectations, false beliefs, Foundation, Framework, dodgy Wiring, distorted glass in Windows and Blueprints all combine to ensure you revert to form, and just like a memory-foam pillow, you spring back to your original shape. Using free-will you are able to change yourself and your life to what you consciously desire, but the minute you get distracted your subconscious covertly manoeuvrers you back to form.

Just as a pilot has to constantly adjust an aeroplane's course in order to maintain the desired destination, your conscious mind has to continuously push against your subconscious autopilot to keep you on track. This is draining, so it's no wonder you eventually give up and allow your subconscious to win the battle. That is until you learn that there is another way, and that is Underpinning.

You now recognise that you can easily say "no" without feeling any of those old uncomfortable feelings. You have every right to go where you want; say what you want and be who you want to be without fearing what others may think or say about you. You are your own judge and you are at peace with your decisions and your behaviours. From now on you will refuse to suffer in silence or say "it's fine" when it is not.

**Questions:**

**What prevents you from moving forward?**

1. Do you believe you are worthy of success?

2. When you make changes, what do your internal underminers say?

3. Who are your external underminers?

4. What are you afraid of when you consider change?

5. What are your external habits?

6. What are your internal habits?

7. What beliefs about yourself restrict you?

8. What do others do that cause intense feelings in you?

9. What are your thoughts when you first wake up?

10. What is your first reaction to a problem?

# BACK TO THE PRESENT

By now you should have a good idea of who you have become and why. You may be aware of your Parent, Adult and Child parts and how your adverse Parent and Child parts interact together to cause drama in your life. You may also be aware of your Adult part and how this is the logical, practical, non-emotional side of you that enables you to solve problems and look at life in a factual and rational way.

You may be aware of your thoughts and whether they come from a negative or positive place; your habits, beliefs and Scaffolding. You may also now know whether you are secure or insecure, assertive, passive, aggressive or passive-aggressive.

You now know where you don't want to be and have taken a look at where you do want to be and perhaps seen some routes to get you there.

You have looked at what holds you back, that Snagging resistance that comes from habits driven by fear of change.

You've seen how your Parent parts try to keep you as you are by demanding that you shouldn't or mustn't change. You may even be able to recognise the Child part that listens to these controlling voices and is too scared to change, and your Adult part that endeavours to balance your Parent and Child parts' thoughts and feelings.

You may be aware that you use Scaffolding to avoid or control feelings of discomfort, and maybe you are now in a place where your Adult part is empowered to continue your journey of change.

Your Blueprint has been reinforced over many years, by many different processes running concurrently, and many new self-esteem growing processes will have to run concurrently in order for permanent change to occur.

Luckily, it will not take so many years to alter your Blueprint.

Often, in counselling, I witness the three steps forward and two steps back effect that happens during change. It's like crossing a bridge from the old place to the new place. You get a short way across the bridge and then get pulled back by your subconscious towards your starting place. This back and forth process repeats throughout the journey, however, every time you are pulled back you don't return quite as far as before, so gradual progress is constantly being made.

One day you find that you spend more time on the other side of the bridge until this becomes your new normal and you begin to forget how it was before.

You notice how much more relaxed you feel. You respond slowly, calmly and assertively to all situations.

Every day you are feeling more and more confident. You are thinking more and more positively and you notice how easy it is to behave assertively.

In the final chapter you'll discover various techniques to enable you to cross that bridge. No one method will get you there on its own. Only by using many of the techniques concurrently will permanent change take place for you.

# BACK TO THE PAST

On this journey so far you've gone way back to look at your family history, systems and rules into which your parents were born and to whom you were subsequently born.

You've explored the environment of your early years and recognised behaviours and conditioning that caused your subconscious to adopt certain beliefs, habits and fears which you have continuously reinforced.

You've looked at how you developed certain expectations of yourself and the world around you which led to repeat cycles and behaviours.

All this fed into your Smart Brain which programmed your thoughts to react automatically so you could think, feel and behave without conscious effort, which is efficient when you have a secure Foundation and prone to faults when your Foundation is insecure.

You may have noticed that with all this conditioning, programming, fear and control you have lost sight of yourself, your sense of self, and this is often where the conflict and inner turmoil lies.

You feel discomfort and use Scaffolding in the guise of control or avoidance, trying to find contentment. These are short-term fixes and when your Tower starts to wobble uncontrollably, you think negatively and feel overwhelmed, you either up the Scaffolding or collapse.

Sometimes it is when you feel at your lowest that you are most empowered to make changes. Your survival instincts drive your determination and motivation which enables you to get on the right path. Along the way you meet resistance from your subconscious (the Snagging) and often revert to form (the memory-foam pillow).

When you learn assertiveness and develop healthy self-esteem you can be in Adult more of the time. In Adult you are better able to change habits, such as negative thinking without feeling fear. You can Re-Parent your inner child with compassion; learn to focus on what you do like about yourself; visualise how you want your life to be and learn to communicate more effectively with yourself and others.

You find that more and more you are becoming more honest, because what you say is not intended to upset or hurt anyone. It is logical and factual and relevant.

If you don't want to do something you simply say "no". If you wish to be on your own or do something by yourself you know you have every right to do so. You have every right to do things the way you wish to without having to explain your self to others or make excuses for your behaviour.

You notice that you give people genuine compliments and now accept compliments by saying "thank you" without embellishing further.

# RETURNING TO YOU
# YOUR UNDERPINNING

What has happened, has happened. Who you are, is who you are. Your Foundation shaped who you are and your conditioning runs deep within your belief system. You were born with a uniqueness that is purely you, but the way you were moulded and brainwashed also became you. The two are inseparable. Like oil and water, essence of you and conditioned you flow around one another and with one another; however, their differences prevent them from combining and their similarities prevent them from separating.

Underpinning is not about taking away the poor-quality materials that were added to your Foundation, but now adding some better-quality materials to make your Foundation stronger and healthier for you.

Being aware of who you are is essential. Before exploring your Foundation you may have been living a life on autopilot. With the benefit of awareness you can now live more consciously and begin to spot various thoughts, feelings and behaviours you display and perhaps recognise where they stem from. If you are aware of what you are doing, you are enabled to change that behaviour.

There will be some elements of yourself that come into your awareness that you may not like but may be able to accept as just being a part of who you are. No one is all good or all bad. In fact, it is probably true that all of us combine good and bad. We have parts of our personalities that we are happy to share with the world and parts that we shy away from or deny even to ourselves.

Change is about discovering your conditioning and challenging it to see if you actually agree with what you are programmed to *should, ought* or *must* do.

It may be that your parents told you it was rude to be late and you've internalised this. However, the genuine you is always late and you spend much time and energy berating yourself about not being good enough.

When you become your own judge and take responsibility for your actions, you can give yourself permission to be late and know that that is okay or you may choose to discover why you are always late and change it if you wish to. If you choose to continue to be late it is not going to suit everyone (especially your parents or your boss) but it will suit you and you can at last be at peace with it. Reaching states of acceptance feels peaceful.

Another important factor in change is looking at your habits; why you started them; how they serve you now, and why you are afraid to stop them.

An example of this could be that you know you have the habit of people pleasing.

You began this behaviour as a child and continued this habit into adult life without question. Now you realise that rather than helping you in life it actually causes other people to take advantage of you or become annoyed with you. You decide this is a habit that no longer serves you well.

However, you then fear changing this habit because your internal voices tell you that people will not like you or will reject you if you do not act as you have always done.

I can assure you that if anyone dislikes you for changing in order to feel better about yourself, they may have some of their own self-awareness work to do.

Underpinning is not an exercise in becoming someone that you are not. It is about feeling more peace and less drama by getting your needs met without putting others down. It is about feeling capable of dealing with whatever life throws your way and feeling that you are deserving of all the good things that life has to offer.

This final chapter will give you the tools, techniques and quality materials needed to Underpin your Foundation. It will help you to learn assertiveness and how to respond to drama in Adult. By doing this you will develop healthy self-esteem.

By challenging habitual negative thinking and your internal underminer, your feelings, behaviours and results will change for the better.

When you are able to treat yourself respectfully you will be indirectly training others to treat you with respect also.

There are also other techniques you can use to create a future on purpose rather than a future that you drift into.

Due to the nature of your Foundation your Tower today will either be very stable, very wobbly or an entire spectrum of in-between.

You have seen how you use Scaffolding to prevent your Tower from crumbling around your feet, and how this explains why, when you use willpower to erase Scaffolding, you find new coping mechanisms to put in its place.

This is why emotional eaters who can lose much weight consciously, through willpower and determination, are then later sabotaged by their subconscious. If the underlying problems that caused the eating-type Scaffolding, are not addressed, then subconscious will revert to form, either by eating again or finding a new type of Scaffolding.

When you carry out Underpinning; when you become assertive, Adult and have healthy self-esteem, a lot of the Scaffolding will naturally fall away on its own.

Yes, there is some Scaffolding that will need extra help, such as heroin addiction for example, but the same principles apply.

## Acceptance

As you discover more about yourself you will become aware of aspects of your personality that you do like and characteristics that challenge you. When you accept all of yourself this becomes part of your new internal Blueprint and of course this means that, if this is happening internally, you will project it externally and become more accepting of other people.

To put it more plainly, you become less judgemental of yourself and others.

This all helps to bring about the 'I'm okay, you're okay' mentality of Adult thinking.

If there are parts of your personality that your parents would have frowned upon and tried to change about you but you can accept them unconditionally, you can be who you know you are without feeling the guilt of the *should, ought* or *must*.

This way of being prevents you thinking: "I will be okay when I'm brighter, kinder, thinner or less reckless," for example, and instead you will experience: "I'm okay just as I am."

With acceptance you will know you will not always fit into the mould your parents created for you and you will be aware that continually trying to squeeze yourself into that mould caused you emotional turmoil and feelings of failure.

Now is the time to accept that you are different in some ways and that this is okay. Your unique qualities are not wrong or bad, they simply do not comply with your conditioning. Embracing your differences frees you from the mould and allows you to feel at peace.

Counselling lends itself to many meaningful sayings, and this one comes to mind now: "What you resist, persists." In other words, when you try to deny your feelings, box them up and push them away, they have a tendency to surface unexpectedly throughout your life causing discomfort and angst when they do. When you embrace your feelings and accept all as is, you live more peacefully.

**Assertiveness**

Assertiveness and self-esteem are not the same. Assertiveness is a way of behaving which can be learned, practised and developed. Self-esteem is a feeling which cannot be learned and practised. When you behave in an assertive way your self-esteem will develop naturally. When you behave in an Adult way instead of a Parent or Child way, self-esteem will grow even stronger.

I tell clients that if they want to have a more supple body they would learn yoga postures and practise them daily. If they want to have healthier self-esteem they would learn assertive behaviours and practise them daily.

Assertive behaviour is when you consider yourself of equal value to others. You are as respectful of your own needs and wants as you are of theirs. You are able to get your own needs met either by asking for what you need or by acting in a way that shows others how you wish to be treated.

When you are passive you are likely to put others before yourself. You are likely to say "yes" when you want to say "no". You are likely to sacrifice your own needs for the needs of others, and sometimes just for the perceived needs of others.

When you are aggressive you are likely to put your needs and wants before others. You are likely to be disparaging towards other people in order to feel okay yourself, and sometimes even use controlling behaviour in order to get your needs met.

Passive-aggressive is when you are actually being aggressive but do it in a gentle way with a smile on your face (as if you are being passive). Much like the grinning assassin you appear to be mild and unassuming and yet your motive is likely to be manipulative to get your needs met. Sarcasm is a well-used form of passive-aggression. Have you ever been called hurtful names and then been told it was only in jest, that you are too sensitive, or that it was said with affection?

Assertive people do not put others down; they do not manipulate or use sarcasm; and they do not control or people please.

An assertive person simply operates for themselves while taking into consideration how their actions may impact on those around them.

They will treat others and themselves with respect. If they do not want to do something they will say so, but they will say "no" because they are genuinely not wanting to do the task and not in order to punish or manipulate someone else.

In effect, they are very straightforward. They are not out to hurt anyone, but equally they are not going to put themselves down. If you are insecure, this way of behaving may sound scary. Listen to that fear. That is your resistance to change.

When you are a passive People Pleaser you may do what someone else wants you to do, or that you think they want you to do, because you are afraid (probably on an irrational Child part level) that the person will cease to like you or may reject you if you do not do what you think they want.

When you people please it can become very confusing, because what one person wants you to do may have an adverse effect on another person, you cannot please both and therefore one may reject you, and you are left with a dilemma.

We've all heard of the saying: "You can please all of the people some of the time, and some of the people all of the time, but not all of the people all of the time."

If you take 200 people and one question, such as do you prefer red or blue? You may get 100 people liking blue and 100 people liking red. The dilemma is, whichever colour you choose, you are likely to alienate 100 people. So you do things like telling all those who like blue that you like blue, and telling all those who like red that you like red. You start to use deceit in order to save yourself from the fear of rejection. Of course, what is likely to happen is that you are found out and all 200 people see you as a fake and you are rejected.

When you operate for yourself you may choose either blue or red, or you may even say you prefer green. Yes, this could alienate 200 people and yet your own integrity remains intact which is important when developing healthy self-esteem.

By growing self-esteem you will feel better about yourself and this makes it easier to feel confident about using Assertive Behaviours. Assertiveness builds self-esteem and self-esteem enables assertiveness.

When you feel okay, you think okay thoughts about yourself. When you think you are okay, you feel okay about yourself. You know you are fair to others and value yourself, and the more you feel this way, the easier (and by that, I mean less scary) it is to stand up for what you believe without the fear of rejection from others.

You realise that those people who reject you for having your own thoughts and opinions whist valuing the thoughts and opinions of others, are people you may choose to spend less time with.

It is very much a chicken and egg situation though. Higher self-esteem lessens the fear you feel when you practise assertiveness, and becoming more assertive grows and develops your self-esteem.

An aggressive person who shouts, swears and bangs doors in order to get their needs met is likely to be experiencing fear. In essence they are trying to scare and intimidate others, in order to control them. They are afraid that if they stop their behaviour they might lose their power over others and then feel out of control.

A passive person may cry and guilt someone into meeting their needs. They are afraid that if they dare ask and are told "no" they may feel rejected and this would seem awful.

An assertive person simply asks for what they need. They either get it or they are told "no", but because they feel okay about themselves they don't take the "no" as a rejection, and remain calm enough to negotiate.

In the Drama Triangle, an assertive person would not feel afraid of the Persecutor; they would simply leave the situation and refuse to experience their rage. Also, an assertive person would not allow themselves to be manipulated by a Victim or Rescuer. You see, you cannot change other people, but you can develop yourself so you are able to step away from abusive behaviour.

If someone criticises an assertive person, rather than going quiet, sulking or crying (Child), the assertive person is more likely to take the wind out of their sails by saying: "Yes, you are right" or "I can hear what you are saying and I don't agree with you," but then not feel the need to explain further.

The assertive person does not experience the hurt or the rage experienced by the person with low self-esteem because they feel okay about themselves inside and therefore the words have less impact.

The words may poke at old emotional wounds or trigger childhood feelings, but the assertive person knows that whatever others say about them is the antagonist's own issues and not theirs.

There are many behaviours you can develop in order to become assertive and, yes, fear is likely to prevent you from risking big sudden changes to your old behaviours. That is okay and entirely normal. By choosing the smallest risk and working on that one first, you may find that a little self-esteem and confidence develops and this may enable you to move on to working on a slightly riskier and scarier habit.

Little steps. Very little steps.

If you had a fear of heights, you'd never tackle a 30 ft ladder straight away. It would be helpful to look at the first rung, step on and off it a for a while until it felt okay, and then move onto the next rung. Eventually you will confidently reach the top of the ladder.

**Self-Esteem**

No one can give you healthy self-esteem and it is not something you can just decide to have. Self-esteem grows when you act assertively.

When you treat yourself with respect and kindness you are setting the benchmark for how you expect other people to treat you.

We are brought up with such beliefs as: "Always put others before yourself" and "treat others as you would expect them to treat you." When we look at just these two examples of conditioning we can easily see why so many of us lived with low self-esteem.

By putting others first it often meant we put ourselves last. We were treating them well and treating ourselves badly. The message we were sending ourselves was that we were not as deserving as them. And, the message we were sending them was that we were not as deserving as them so they didn't have to treat us well either.

People with low self-esteem feel that other people are better equipped to deal with life than they are. Their thoughts are generally negative – along the lines of: "Oh, I can never do it as well as them." It's the 'they're okay, I'm not okay' position and it comes from the type of low self-esteem that produces a passive personality. This passiveness tends to lead to Child feelings of vulnerability, fear, helplessness and generally feeling incapable of dealing with life.

The other type of person who suffers with low self-esteem is the boastful "look at me and see what I've done" person, who is sometimes down-putting and sometimes aggressive.

Some people look at these forceful and intimidating people and think they must have high self-esteem in order to behave with such confidence. But this is not so.

Anyone who has to boast themselves up or put others down in order to feel better about themselves certainly does not have high self-esteem. They are operating from the 'I'm okay, you're not okay' perspective.

When someone has healthy self-esteem they have no need to shout about how great they are or behave aggressively. They are simply their own judge. If they feel they have done okay, that they have been heard and heard others without putting themselves or others down, then they are okay (and so are others).

Not convinced? Let's consider children.

They are naturally narcissistic and the world revolves around them, and  rightly so. Cognitively they only have the ability to view the world from their own perspective and assume everyone else sees, experiences and feels the exact same way they do. It is not until they develop a theory of mind that this begins to change.

Insecure children  can be clingy and shy and learn that it is safest to be passive and put others before themselves. Insecure children can also be avoidant and dominating and learn that it is safest to be at the front of the line and bully-ish. The child's Foundation will have a great deal of influence in determining these types of Attachment styles.

Secure children are more likely to happily share toys with other children, are not afraid to ask for a toy, and will wait or play with another toy until it is their turn. They will expect to get their turn, however.

Your self-esteem developed by way of the messages you were given as a child. These messages included how your parents viewed children in general and you in particular. If they believed that you should be seen and not heard then you did not learn to be assertive. Equally, if they believed you were the best and should be put first, you did not learn to be assertive.

Self-esteem forms in childhood, in those Foundations and, of course, even before this in your Groundwork. You were probably born with a pre-disposition (like a seed of self-esteem) and this germinated and grew.

Parents with healthy self-esteem have children with healthy self-esteem. The same pattern is true of parents with low self-esteem. Learned behaviour, conditioning, the Metaphorical Mirror and genetics ensure this.

Much of what we teach our children about themselves is done subconsciously out of our awareness. A parent with healthy self-esteem will automatically behave in ways that teach their child that they are respected and so are others.

If you are planning to have children, this is the greatest motivation for developing your own self-esteem.

For those of us who already have children perhaps we can offer ourselves some compassion and accept that we did the best we could with what we had available to us emotionally and intellectually at that time.

Healthy self-esteem is when you feel okay about you, you trust your thoughts, your feelings and your behaviours, and you value yourself and you value others. I'm okay, you're okay. You take responsibility for your behaviour, even when you mess up.

If someone has low self-esteem, they may be passive and allow others to use them, walk over them or abuse them or they might be hostile, aggressive, boastful and forceful.

Someone with low self-esteem may be judgemental of others and believe themselves to be right and others to be wrong, or they may criticise themselves and believe others are right and they are wrong.

Someone with healthy self-esteem believes in themselves and trusts themselves.

They are also aware that although their viewpoint, perspective or filter is correct for them, other people may see things in a very different way and that their perspective may be true for them.

They respect their view point and they respect that of other people.

Here are examples of people with low self-esteem (passive and aggressive) and healthy self-esteem (assertive) and how one scenario might play out in three different ways.

Bob has low self-esteem and it manifests itself by him being a passive person. His Smart Brain interprets that others know better than him and his opinion is not of value or as valuable or trustworthy than other people's (You're okay, I'm not okay).

His wife says she is leaving him because she is fed up with taking responsibility for everything.

Bob thinks to himself: "Well, I can't make decisions because I might get it wrong and she always seems to know what's best."

Through his Windows he sees that he is not as worthy as other people and can understand why she doesn't want to be with him any more.

He always believed she was too good for him and would leave him and now he has created a self-fulfilling-prophecy.

Bob can see that his wife is right and feels that he has been a rubbish husband and allows her to take the house, the children, the dog and their savings, because he feels so guilty (Victim/Rescuer).

He sleeps on a friend's sofa and wallows in self-pity because he knows that he is useless and destined to have nothing. He feels incapable of changing the situation and undeserving of more.

Bert also has low self-esteem but this manifests in an aggressive way. His wife tells him she is going to leave him because she can no longer tolerate his angry outbursts and door slamming.

Bert shouts at his wife that she infuriates him with her nagging and believes it's no wonder he reacts the way he does (Persecutor/Victim). His Wiring interprets that she makes him behave that way and it's all her fault.

Through Bert's Windows he sees that the world is a hostile place and everyone is out to do him wrong and take advantage of him (I'm okay, you're not okay).

He refuses to leave the family home and begins to smash it up in rage. His wife calls the police and has him removed. The police impose a restraining order on Bert which reinforces his belief that everyone is out to get him.

George has secure Foundations. His parents believed in him, listened to what he had to say and although they didn't always agree with him they respected and valued his opinions. George has grown up with the belief that he is okay and so are other people. He has healthy self-esteem.

His wife tells him she is going to leave him because she no longer loves him. George is upset by this news and shares his feelings with his wife, making her aware this is a shock to him (Assertive).

George doesn't think he is the most attractive or romantic man but he feels that he has been a loving and generous husband and can't understand what has gone wrong. He opens up a dialogue with his wife about how he feels and he respects what she says in return.

He tells her he feels angry, shocked, confused and upset, but he does not blame her for the way he feels. He doesn't like feeling this way, but he knows that logically (Adult) he has been an okay husband.

His wife is adamant there is nothing he or she can do to save the marriage. George would prefer to be with his wife, but also knows he will be okay on his own and so will she (I'm okay, you're okay).

In all three scenarios the marriage is over, but George has been able to regulate his emotions and the situation is resolved without regretful actions. George's behaviour was also the one most likely to resolve the marital issues had his wife been open to this.

By learning and practising a range of assertive behaviours every day over a period of time, your level of self-esteem will increase further.

## Assertive Behaviour

Here are some ideas to learn, practise and develop:

Practise saying NO

Spend more time around people who support and encourage you

Spend less time around people who put you down or tease you

Say sorry less

Express what you would like without violating the rights of others

Be respectful of yourself and of others

By respecting yourself you are likely to be respected by others

People pleasing results in you and others feeling hurt

Do what is right for you, even when others disagree

By being true to yourself you feel better about yourself

When you feel better about yourself you have better relationships with others

Do things because they are meaningful to you and not because you should/must

When you sacrifice your rights you are likely to be resentful of others

Let others know how you feel. Not letting them know could be selfish

If you don't say how you feel, others cannot choose to change their behaviour

Be Self-ful rather than Self-less or Self-ish

Other people react and respond to how you behave and not to how you feel

You have a right to respect and so do others

When someone is mean to you or others, it speaks volumes about them, not you

Notice your fears when considering taking these risks, be curious about them

Take time to respond to other people's words or behaviours

Swap instant reaction for a considered response

Pause and think before you act

Treat yourself equally to others

Try saying: "I feel………when you do………" rather than "you make me feel like….."

Apologise and hold your hands up only when you have made a mistake

You have as much right to your own time, interests and friends as anyone else

Your feelings are important and valid, and so are other people's

Your perspective may be different from others', and that is okay

When you do what is right for you, you are always right for you

Your most important relationship is with yourself

Treat your body as you would want a loved one to treat theirs

Speak to yourself with kindness and compassion

Become aware of negative thinking and challenge your thoughts

Learn to eat well, sleep well, exercise and relax

Be kind to others and yourself

Take responsibility for yourself

Write down a few things you are grateful for every day

Focus on what you like about yourself and others

Focus on what you want your life to look like

Enjoy this journey of discovery

Become aware of and change your internal dialogue if needed

Challenge thoughts you have about yourself

Discover the beliefs you hold and challenge them

Repeatedly tell yourself the things you want to believe about yourself such as "I am good enough".

Ask for what you need

Do the things you want to do rather than those you think you should do

Notice and be curious about any uncomfortable feelings that surface – whereabouts in your body are the feelings; imagine what the feelings look like; are they still or moving etc.

Volunteer and do random good deeds

Be grateful for what you already have

Accept compliments with a simple "thank you"

And finally, an important note to People Pleasers. Rather than going ahead and doing things for people because you think they want you to or because you think it will be good for them, make a point of asking them first if they would like you to do this and then respect their reply.

**Emotional First Aid Box**

Create a box which holds lots of different ideas that you can do to comfort, soothe or distract yourself. When you are having a 'wobbly Tower' day it is often easier to reach for old Scaffolding than to think of other ways to calm yourself.

This type of First Aid Box will provide you with extra resources that you may not be able to think of when you are feeling vulnerable, overwhelmed, lonely, anxious, depressed etc.

Write each suggestion on a separate piece of paper and place them in an actual box or keep the ideas in list form where it is easily accessible.

Items you may include treating yourself to a bought coffee or a new item of clothing; an hour reading or watching easy television; take a bath or shower; walk in nature; practise Mindfulness or Meditation; do a chore such as digging or cleaning; phone or meet a friend; spend an hour on a hobby; make a comfy space out of cushions and soft toys; watch a Disney film whilst tucked up on the sofa; write down how you feel; go for a walk or run; think of five things you are grateful for; cook; draw or paint; cycle; play up-lifting music, dance or sing.

Keeping a journal can also be really useful. Rather than a diary, this is a private book where you can write down any thoughts, feelings, dreams, memories, significant events or conversations, as and when they arise. If no words come, a journal is a great place to draw or just scribble.

## Positive thinking

The chapter on Snagging explained that when you feel something very strongly you have a propensity to believe it to be true – the angry person feeling rage in The Traffic Jam was certain the traffic had made her angry.

It also stated how your thoughts direct your feelings, and that the angry driver in The Traffic Jam was probably thinking something like: "I just knew I'd get held up today. This road is terrible for traffic. It's just my luck that it would be worse than ever today." This kind of negative inner self-talk will lead to negative feelings such as anger.

There are times when negative thinking serves a useful purpose, such as if you leave your home and start to think that you could have left a candle burning. You may begin thinking about all the problems it could cause if you had and, with images in your mind of your home on fire, you turn around and double-check that the candle is out.

However, when you think: "I wonder how my trip to Scotland will go? I hope there isn't too much traffic. What if there is and what if it's foggy and what if I can't brake quick enough and end up in a pile-up?" Your thinking spirals out of control and causes you to feel bad.

Even writing this scenario causes my anxiety to rise and I'm not even planning a trip to Scotland. (I live in East Anglia, so please substitute another long-distance destination if you happen to live in or near Scotland, or in another country.)

This kind of negative thinking causes negative emotions and it does not serve a useful purpose. The likely outcome is that you worry so much about the trip that you call it off or can't enjoy looking forward to it. This line of thinking or, to put it another way, imagining pretend situations is not going to change the traffic or the weather between here and Scotland. It is only going to cause you undue stress.

If you had thoughts like: "I'm really looking forward to my trip to Scotland. I love long drives and passing through different counties. Just getting away fills me with a sense of freedom and relaxation," you then begin to feel excited about the trip and happy that you're able to have that experience.

Notice that nothing has changed about the actual trip, only your thinking about it. By changing the way you think about it, you have changed your feelings about it.

You, like all of us, were biologically built so that what you think impacts how you feel, and how you feel regulates your hormones. Depending on whether you feel content or stressed impacts on the amount of happy or stress chemicals released into your body. And this impacts on your behaviour.

For example, when you feel anxious your heart races and your palms may become sweaty due to stress chemicals released into your body to prepare you for the stressful event (fight, flight or freeze).

Once your physical body has responded according to your feelings you are in a position to act on how you feel and then you get a result. In the negative version of the Scotland trip, the way you're likely to behave is to stay at home or feel stressed before the journey and therefore the result is that you're likely to miss out on a wonderful experience.

What is more, by staying at home and not travelling you have not proven to your brain that the trip to Scotland could be enjoyable and, so next time a similar trip comes up, you are likely to have reinforced your negative thinking and therefore decide not to go.

Your thoughts create a cycle of events. When you think positively, you feel positive, your body reacts accordingly, this impacts on your behaviour, you get a good result, and this result reinforces your positive thinking. This is your Cycle for Success.

When you have negative thoughts, you feel negative emotions, your body releases negative hormones, you behave according to how you feel, you get bad results, and these results reinforce your negative thinking. This is your Cycle of Doom.

You can choose to use this cycle to create your Cycle for Success or to enter into a Cycle of Doom.

The choice is yours.

**Cycle for Success or Cycle of Doom**

**Breaking the Cycle of Doom**

To break the habit of subconscious, automatic negative thinking and begin to think more positively there are a few conscious techniques that can be practised.

## 1. Challenging thoughts

You have the power to change your thinking by taking control of the thought and attaching a different meaning to an event.

It is helpful to break down this technique into stages in order to practise it and create a new habit.

First, spend a week just noticing when you think negatively. You may notice that you were in the kitchen cooking dinner when you started thinking: "This food is going to be awful. I'm a terrible cook. No one will eat it and they'll think I'm stupid."

Ouch! That's some powerful negative self-talk.

Now write it down and for the first week this is all you have to do. Notice when you think negatively and write it down because this encourages awareness (there are worksheets with examples at the end of this chapter).

On the second week repeat this, and add the situation you were in and notice how the thoughts made you feel. Write all this down during the second week (if you feel that weeks are too long, try replacing the word *week* with *day*).

During week three write down the negative thought, the situation, the emotion this created, whereabouts in your body you felt it and how did it feel.

Week four is a repeat of week three and add how you behaved because of how you felt.

Week five is a repeat of week four and add the result that you achieved due to your behaviour.

This may seem a lengthy process, but you have spent many years learning how to think negatively and it may take a couple of months of practise before you begin to notice a change to your habit of automatic negative thinking.

During week six continue as before but when you write down the thought and the feeling it created, ask yourself how true you believe your thoughts and feelings to be between 0% and 100%.

It may be that you are planning a trip to Scotland and have been thinking about how dangerous the journey there could be and are feeling anxious about going.

Maybe you feel 90% confident that your thoughts are justified and 95% confident that your feelings reinforce this.

Next, challenge your thoughts with facts. How often have you or others made this trip on the same roads? How likely is an accident? What is the weather generally like at that time of year?

You may discover that 4% of travellers on that journey encounter any kind of problem and at that time of year the weather is dry and clear 80% of the time (unlikely in Scotland :) ).

Armed with this information you are in a position to make a more realistic judgement (using your Adult part). Look back at your thinking and re-evaluate it. Maybe you now consider the thought of that journey being dangerous as only 15% true and you may notice that this reflects on your feeling-state and you are now more relaxed.

Week seven. Repeat week six and add the behaviour and result after the re-evaluation. You can compare these with your behaviours and results from week five.

Continue repeating week seven until you feel that challenging negative thoughts has become your new habit.

There is a bonus worksheet included at the end of this chapter especially for Mind Readers and Fortune Tellers (those who negatively predict what other people are thinking about them and foretell forthcoming events as doomed).

Use these sheets to predict what you think people are thinking about you or what you think they expect of you and then ask them if this is true.

When you have an up-coming event or trip, write down how you foretell it will be, and once it has actually happened go back to your prediction and compare it with the reality.

## 2. Changing behaviours

The diagram, Cycle for Success or Cycle of Doom shows how your thinking creates feelings and these feelings create behaviours and results.

If you find it too difficult to challenge your negative thinking in order to change your thoughts, feelings, behaviours and results you may wish to try changing your behaviours instead. By changing your negative behaviours, despite your thoughts you automatically change your results. This feeds positively back into your thoughts and therefore naturally changes the Cycle of Doom to the Cycle for Success without the need to challenge your thinking.

This is how:

You may wake up in the morning and think: "I'm dreading today. The boss will be in a bad mood and will probably be mean to me." Maybe you are unable to challenge or positively change these thoughts. As a result you feel down and unmotivated and drag yourself into work. You don't speak to anyone, you look miserable and you work slowly. Your boss sees how unmotivated you are and tells you to buck up your ideas. Your negative behaviour got results and these negative results reinforced your thoughts of: "I knew it would all go wrong."

Changing your behaviour may look like this:

You may wake up in the morning and think: "I'm dreading today. The boss will be in a bad mood and will probably be mean to me." You begin to feel down and unmotivated, but you are now aware that this is the start of the Cycle of Doom. Today you decide to do something different. You decide to get straight in the shower, and as you feel the water flowing over you and you start to sing. You smile to yourself. You get ready for work quickly and leave the house. As you walk you stand taller, pull your shoulders back, hold your head up, say "hello" to people and smile. This may not have been how you felt like behaving this morning, but now that you are, you begin to notice a change in your thinking and in your feeling-state.

By the time you get to work you are thinking more positively and feeling more motivated. Your boss congratulates you on a good day's work.

Motivational speaker Linda Larsen describes, in her 12 Secrets to High Self-Esteem, a time that she recognised the pattern working as the success cycle.

She was driving through a toll booth in no particular feeling-state, and stopped to pay the toll. The cashier turned to her with a big smile on his face and in an excited tone he said: "Hello, how lovely to see you," as if he knew her. She was so taken aback that she smiled at him and said something like: "Well, it's lovely to see you too, what makes you so happy?" He replied that happy, friendly people turned up at his toll booth every day.

149

Linda could almost imagine him getting up in the morning thinking excitedly: "I'm going to work and I'm going to meet lots of happy, friendly people today. I'm so lucky to have such a great job." He feels happy and upbeat on the way to work and excited about the day ahead. His behaviour towards people is happy and welcoming and the result is that people are happy and friendly in return, which feeds back into his thoughts about how wonderful his customers are.

I wonder how things would play out if he got up in the morning thinking (in an Eeyore-style of voice): "Another day at work. How monotonous. It's so boring and I feel so old and grumpy." My guess is that the way he'd greet his customers would reflect how he felt and the results produced by his behaviour would reinforce his negative thoughts.

### 3. Using the A, B, C, D method to change negative thinking

The A, B, C, D method works on the same theory as the Challenging Thoughts method, but is simplified.

A is the Adverse event that happens, such as your friend not returning your text.

B is the Belief you attach to this event: "I must have done something to upset her and she hates me."

C is the Consequence of your thoughts. You feel alone, abandoned, rejected, and hurt.

D is for all the Different possibilities of why she didn't return your call. She was busy, she didn't receive your text, she did reply and you missed it.

By creating different possibilities you are changing your thoughts and this changes your emotions.

## 4. Re-tracking thoughts

When you worry about things that are not within your control, such as: "What if I catch the Corona Virus? What if I run out of food? How long will this go on for?" your imagination will naturally go to the next stage, of creating unpleasant images and feelings until you are motivated to act; however, because you have no way of resolving these questions, you remain feeling anxious about them.

Anxiety is the normal and natural emotion you feel when you don't know the outcome to something and so you worry about it. You think you have no control over the outcome and feel afraid of the many negative scenarios you create in your imagination of how the outcome may play out.

In these situations the outcome is not going to be affected by your worrying. Your worries are only going to cause you discomfort and serve no useful purpose.

Earlier in this chapter we looked at challenging negative thinking by writing down your experiences in order to see how your thoughts impact your feelings and behaviours. During this exercise you would have become more aware of your thinking and more able to 'catch' those negative thoughts.

Once you are aware of those thoughts it is easier to notice your cycles. If you are prone to negative thinking this is a quick method of changing your thoughts and therefore feeling better.

"What if I get the virus?" This is not in itself a negative thought, but when your imagination automatically runs with this thought and embellishes it negatively it is. "This might happen and that might happen, and oh no, how awful that would be," and you would naturally begin to feel anxious.

I like to think of a negative thought as a runaway train racing off down a track. I imagine a runaway train, racing away down a track and gaining speed towards a dark tunnel. I call it a Negative Train of Thought.

**Negative Train of Thought**

Once you are aware of the train on the track, you can say (out loud if you like) "Stop!"

And now imagine a new track going off at an angle and your train going off down this line instead.

At the end of this new line is a store cupboard containing many neutral and happy thoughts that are individual to you. You get to create your own store cupboard. Among other things, my store cupboard contains my clients, metaphorically of course.

Here is an example of how it worked for me:

I was walking my dog and not really thinking about anything in particular. Then I noticed the fog across a field, and off went my Negative Train off Thought as if it had a turbo engine. I thought: "Fog - daughter - driving to work - can't see - red brake lights - accident – ambulance." You can imagine how I started to feel. Panic and terror mainly. "Helen Stop!" I said. "Now re-track," and I visualised my train going down a new track towards my store cupboard.

I started to think: "Who am I seeing today? What did we talk about last time? What might we discuss today?"

As I cannot think of two different things at the same time, I no longer thought about the fog and therefore my imagination no longer created the horrific scenario and as a result my anxiety decreased rapidly.

Just because we can imagine scenarios vividly and create corresponding intense feelings, does not mean it is reality. We are making it up. We are not able to predict the future.

However, focusing on the negative could have inadvertently caused it to come true.

For example, if I had continued with my line of irrational thinking, my anxiety would have escalated and my next course of action would have been to telephone my daughter to see if she was okay.

My call may have created an accident if it distracted her from driving.

Your imagination is probably the most powerful tool in your tool box and you can see how easily it could be used unhelpfully. There are also many ways to use it helpfully. More about this later.

Sometimes a client tells me they just cannot stop worrying and sometimes they don't want to because it helps them think of solutions to problems (classic Snagging).

I suggest that these people select a 'worry time', perhaps an hour a day between, say, 6pm and 7pm, in which to worry. If they have a worry crop up during the day, they can simply note the worry and come back to it later at the designated time.

**Adult**

You already have an Adult part. In the section discussing TA you recognised your Parent, Adult and Child parts.

Within the Drama Triangle, the Parent parts are represented by Persecutor and Rescuer at the top of the triangle, the Child part is represented by Victim at the bottom point of the triangle, and Adult runs along the dotted line in the middle cutting through the drama with logic, fact and rational thinking.

Your Adult part developed from your own experiences and knowledge that you took on board as you journeyed through life. From those earliest first steps, through education, interaction with others, television learning, activities and arriving at now.

Adult is logical, rational, factual, planning and problem-solving. It is neither aggressive or passive. It is assertive. When you are in Adult there is no drama. You are not taking the role of Persecutor, Rescuer or Victim. You feel emotionally sound and secure.

Often people feel in Adult at work (if they feel confident and equal to others at work). Yet, these same Adult workers, can sometimes feel mainly in Parent and Child at home. Adult is independent and open.

If you are in Adult you will want to be with the person you've fallen in love with and you will know that, although upset and sad if they left you, you would be okay on your own. You are in the relationship because you want to be and not because you need to be.

Although you have this Adult part you also have Parent and Child parts and can easily get drawn into them especially when life becomes tricky. If your childhood was spent living within a Drama Triangle, your starting default position will be either Persecutor, Rescuer or Victim.

The Adapted Child part is conditioned with the *should, ought* and *must* commands of the Critical and Nurturing Parent parts. Adapted Child was created within you to feel safe in environments that you had no control over.

Free Child is reckless, spontaneous and free-spirited. You have some of this too. These parts are emotional and vulnerable. The Adult part is factual, logical, rational, problem-solving and balanced. It operates in the here and now.

The stronger the Adult part is, the more peaceful, balanced and secure the person feels.

Parent and Child parts tend to work together and reinforce one another. Say you are feeling neutral, neither one thing or another, and your holiday flight is cancelled at short notice because of a storm. What do you think and feel, and how do you behave?

Perhaps this. Maybe your first thought is: "Typical! This always happens to me. Whenever I plan anything nice it goes wrong (Child (Victim)). Well obviously things always go wrong. It's not as if you deserve anything nice. You're nothing but trouble (Critical Parent (Persecutor))." You feel disappointed (Child). "Okay, so what are we going to do about this? (Adult). I'll give the travel agent a ring and see if I can arrange another flight and reschedule my work or cut the holiday a little shorter (Adult)." You make the call and can go on holiday two days later than planned. Inner voice thinks: "I'm angry that the holiday is shorter (Child)." Later: "It's okay, we can still do this and that, and it will be a fantastic time." (Nurturing Parent (Rescuer) comforting inner child and distracting them with thoughts of nicer things).

You start to feel excited and can't wait to go on holiday (Free Child). You smile and dance around the kitchen with the dog (Free Child). Looking at these inner components it is easy to see why different situations can bring forward or *trigger* these different parts of our psyche.

When things go wrong in a Tower-shaking kind of way, such as redundancy, divorce, death or illness, our vulnerable Child part is triggered and becomes stronger.

Sometimes clients say to me that they had felt confident and mature and able to cope with anything that life threw their way, but since a particular event they seem unable to do any of the things as they did before. They feel unsure and incapable.

When a person's security is rocked, they feel insecure and their Child is triggered. When a person feels out of control, their Parent part comes forward to try to take control. When a person resolves problems by being pro-active, their Adult part becomes stronger.

An insecure grown-up will become lost in the drama and feeling-states of Child and Parent and their Adult may be difficult to reach. A secure grown-up will still feel sad or upset in a crisis but their stronger Adult part will be more able to regulate these emotions and find a logical solution more quickly.

When you learn to be assertive, Adult grows stronger. When you practise thinking rationally about the facts of a situation rather than dwelling on negative imaginations and irrational feelings, Adult grows stronger.

## Re-Parenting

Your Foundation and Framework (your parents and their behaviour) shaped the person you are today. Looking objectively and without judgement, perhaps you can acknowledge that they treated you in a way they believed to be in your best interests, and you carry the symptoms of unintended collateral damage.

Mainly, parents parent subconsciously, and therefore without awareness, according to the way in which they were parented.

Which reminds me of this poem by Philip Larkin:

They fuck you up, your mum and dad.
They may not mean to, but they do.
They fill you with the faults they had
And add some extra, just for you.

But they were fucked up in their turn
By fools in old-style hats and coats,
Who half the time were soppy-stern
And half at one another's throats.

Man hands on misery to man.
It deepens like a coastal shelf.
Get out as early as you can,
And don't have any kids yourself.

Well, that's one way of looking at it. You cannot go back and change the past because what happened, happened. However, what is within your control is how you are from this day forward.

As well as learning assertiveness, growing healthy self-esteem and becoming more Adult and less Parent and Child, another part of the Underpinning process involves Re-Parenting. By this I mean treating yourself now in a way that would have been preferable to your mental health when you were a child.

Maybe you heard phrases like: "You've made your bed, so you can lay in it," "don't care was made to care," "children should be seen and not heard," "stop crying or I'll give you something to cry about," "you useless article, what were you thinking?"

When a child is brought up by parents who use this type of language, the child internalises the words and the meaning they (the child) place on the words. The child then uses these words when talking to their self via their internal dialogue, and continue to do this long after they grow up and leave their parents.

You may start to be aware of how you speak to yourself, your inner self-talk, so to speak.

When you stub your toe, do you say to yourself : "You stupid idiot, you should look where you're going?" Or, do you say: "Oh dear, let's take a look at that and make sure it's okay?" When you make a mistake do you criticise yourself or speak to yourself with compassion and kindness? When you look in the mirror do you put yourself down and pull yourself apart or do you kindly accept yourself just as you are? Are you frustrated by your flaws and weaknesses, or do you celebrate your individuality?

If you were brought up with conditional love you would have internalised this, and consider that you will only be content when you are thin enough, successful enough, clever enough, pretty enough, fast enough, and so on.

These children were taught that only when they were 'good enough' would they feel accepted and when they were not good enough they feel would feel rejected. These conditions of worth result in how much or how little you value yourself. Do you feel acceptable or do you consider yourself to be a reject?

The way you speak to yourself would be heavily influenced by the way your parents spoke to you. Remember, they held up that

Metaphorical Mirror and told you who you were and what you were worth, using verbal and non-verbal communication.

When you Re-Parent yourself you start to treat yourself as you would treat a vulnerable young child now. Would you be kind and compassionate to a tearful 4-year-old or reprimand them?

If you would reprimand them you may have a bit more work to do before Re-Parenting yourself.

Now is the time to start treating yourself in the way you have always deserved to be treated, with kindness and love. Would you treat a child the way you treat yourself? Would you speak to them the way you speak to yourself? Would you be so mean and intolerant of them as your are of you? Usually, at this point, the answer is: "No, of course not." Then there is often a big "but". Many clients tell me that of course they wouldn't speak to a young child the way they speak to themselves; however, they are grown-ups now and *should* know better.

Yes, you may be a grown-up now, but when you internalised this way of speaking to yourself you were a child. You learned how to speak to yourself by listening to your parents; you formed a habit and have continued to speak to yourself in this way without questioning how it impacts you.

When you speak to yourself in a derogatory way you are not showing yourself respect and therefore you are not going to feel deserving of a better life and others are more likely to treat you disrespectfully too.

In a similar way, when I encourage a client to think of their self as a small child experiencing the criticism, abuse or bullying they experienced as a child, they will sometimes say they do not like their child-self because they should have done something about the situation and didn't.

Maybe they should have been better behaved or ran away or told someone or simply objected to their treatment. Really? As a child did you really have the power, the strength or the resources to act in this way? Maybe it was sheer terror that prevented you from doing these things. Whatever the reason, the fact is that sometimes, whether it is habit, belief or conditioning, it is difficult to feel compassion for yourself.

The great news is, that although it is sometimes difficult to feel compassion for yourself you may be able to feel compassion for someone else, and you can use that idea to shift the way you talk to yourself.

The first part of this change is to become aware of how you speak to yourself. During the next few weeks, you may begin to recognise times when you are having an internal conversation with yourself and notice the words and tone you use.

At this stage just notice. Almost like noticing a cloud passing by, just notice it, acknowledge it and allow it to drift by.

Over a short period of time you may begin to be more aware of how you are with yourself. It is at this point you could ask yourself is this how you would speak to a young child?

When you were young your parents spoke to you and you experienced different feelings according to what they said, how it was said and how you interpreted it.

As you grew up, your inner child remained within you. The negative and positive feelings you experienced as a child are still within you. This is the TA Child part. Your inner dialogue of control is your inner Parent part that still parents your inner child. If your parents were insecure it is likely that your inner Parent has more of the adverse qualities of Critical and Nurturing Parent, such as down-putting and smothering.

It is also therefore more likely that your inner child experiences more of the adverse affects of Adapted and Free Child, such as fear and recklessness.

Although you are a grown-up now you continue to speak to your inner child in the way your parents spoke to you as a child.

Using your Adult, you can now learn to speak to your inner child with love and compassion, by tapping into the favourable qualities of your Parent parts, such as protecting yourself, encouraging yourself to try new things, caring for yourself and standing up for yourself. Your inner child is going to take a while to catch up with this change and is going to feel all those old familiar feelings such as fear and guilt, when your inner Parent voice starts to change.

I wonder if you tried any of the suggested Assertive Behaviour ideas and felt those familiar feelings surface? Did you practise saying "no" and feel the guilt, or try asking for what you needed and experienced the fear of rejection? These feelings came directly from your inner child.

When you Re-Parent yourself you might imagine your inner child as you as a child standing beside you now. When you sense your old familiar feelings, you can now recognise them as coming from your child-self and speak to him or her as a secure parent would. Your Adult self will be able to resource this behaviour. You speak to your child-self with love, kindness and compassion and with gentle encouragement. If you notice criticism, humiliation or shame, you are using old habits. You will initially hear all the old familiar Parent voices chirping away (internal underminers). Simply thank them for their input and tell them that you are now doing things differently. Continue speaking to your child-self as you would any other young child. Eventually those adverse Parent voices will quieten.

This may feel uncomfortable, unnatural and even fraudulent to begin with, and I urge you to keep practising it, until it becomes second nature. Your inner child should begin to experience the spontaneous, joyful and creative qualities of your Free Child.

On discovering who you are and how you came to be, think, feel and behave, you might start to notice certain difficult emotions surfacing.

These may include grief for your lost childhood or anger towards your parents. You may begin to remember certain abusive or traumatic events which perhaps seemed normal to you at the time but now, on reflection, are questionable experiences.

If the latter is the case, you may be able to work through them yourself or with a close friend, but if you are struggling I would recommend that you find a qualified counsellor to help you work through these feelings. All feelings that surface are absolutely valid and normal and it may be a good idea to notice and acknowledge them.

When we look at the Parent, Adult, Child model of psychology, it is the Parent who tells us who we *should* be, *must* be or *ought* to be, our Adult is logical and rational and finds a balance; the Child is the emotional part, so if you are experiencing difficult feelings based on your childhood experiences it  could be that your Child part  is screaming  out  to  be  listened  to  and  this  is  recommended.

As well as the Re-Parenting technique, 'Letters, not to send', 'Story Telling' and 'Self Comforting' can also be helpful:

**Letters, not to send**

If doing these exercises causes difficult emotions to surface, letter writing can often help your Child part express their feelings in a safe way.

It gives your Child part a chance to finally be heard – by you.

Write letters from your child-self to the grown-up that you feel let you down all that time ago. Really try to let rip here. It is quite safe because the letters are not meant for sending. It is a way of expressing your inner child's feelings and allowing them to be heard by you. Notice any resistance (Snagging) you have to writing these letters. How difficult is it to pick up a pen and paper and write down your feelings? Are you tempted to make excuses not to do the exercise or as you write, to make excuses for the grown-up's behaviour?

Yes, of course, most of the time these grown-ups were doing the very best they could for you given their own abilities, experiences and knowledge, but this is not about why they behaved as they did, this is about how you as a child experienced these behaviours. What was it like for you?

## Story Telling

Another method is to write a story about a child telling a grown-up what happened to them and how they felt when it happened. The grown-up listens and responds with kindness and compassion. The known, but unspoken twist to this story is that both the grown-up and the child are you. In the story, the grown-up is maternal or paternal towards the child and listens to every word whilst being 100% supportive of the child. Allow the grown-up to tell the child how wrong it was that the child suffered in the way they did, and allow the child to fully reveal what it was like for them to experience the feelings of their early years.

## Self-Comforting

Another way to heal your inner child is to comfort yourself in a childlike way or a way you would have liked to have been comforted when you felt hurt or afraid as a child.

If you feel sadness, you may want to cuddle up on the sofa with a Disney film, blanket and cuddly toy. If you feel anger, you may want to drive into the countryside and scream at the top of your voice or beat up a pillow or stomp around releasing that anger into the floor. Perhaps your child-self had favourite television programmes, food or things they enjoyed. Simply rubbing your arms as if giving yourself a hug and telling yourself: "It will all be okay," can be a very effective way of comforting yourself.

Now maybe a good time to allow your inner child the time and space to do these things. With the internet it is easy to find children's programmes of many years ago. Perhaps you have Lego, jigsaw puzzles or paints for your children or grandchildren to play with that you can escape into.

Really allow your inner child to play, and to be expressed, heard and comforted.

Once you have acknowledged and perhaps dealt with any surfacing emotions you may be ready to continue growing your self-esteem.

When you have spent years not liking yourself and telling yourself you are not okay, this is reflected not only in the way you speak to yourself but in the way you feel about yourself.

The most important relationship in your life is the relationship you have with yourself, so now is as good a time as any to begin having a great relationship with yourself.

**What I like about myself**

What *do* you like about yourself? Nothing? Really? Is there something about your personality that you like? No? Okay, think of someone who likes you or loves you, and write down what you think they would say about you.

Once you have done this exercise regarding your personality move onto to how you see yourself physically.

So, again, what do you like about yourself? How about your little toe on your left foot? Your ears? Your eyes? Your hair? Your skin? Your good health? Your knees perhaps? If you really can't focus on anything positive about your looks I suggest covering up your mirrors. Seriously! What you can't see you won't criticise, and what you are not thinking about is not affecting you emotionally.

In Linda Larsen's 12 Steps to Higher Self Esteem, she suggests that you create a 'finest and best' list. This is a list of any positive qualities you have ever been able to recognise in yourself. If you have ever once felt you looked attractive, then it can go on this list because at your 'finest and best' you can confidently say you looked attractive. Once the list is written make two copies and have one by your bed to read before you go to sleep and first thing in the morning and keep the other in your wallet or phone so that you can read it if you are ever waiting in a queue or for an appointment.

When you read each line imagine you are back there in the moment, feel what you felt, hear what you heard and see what you saw.

When you focus on what you like about yourself, you begin to like yourself more. When you focus on what you dislike about yourself, you dislike yourself more.

Perhaps, rather than thinking negatively about yourself, such as: "I am too fat and I should be thin," how about telling yourself: "I am slim and I'd like to be slimmer." It cuts out the negativity.

You were brainwashed into believing negative messages about yourself and you have been reinforcing these messages for years. Now, it is going to take a certain amount of re-brainwashing yourself in order to reprogram your Smart Brain to recognise positive messages about yourself.

**Mindfulness**

When you think of the past (even yesterday) you can feel depressed about not being able to change what happened. When you look to the future (even tomorrow) you can feel anxious about not knowing what will happen. It is often more peaceful to live in the moment. To bring your thoughts to NOW, right now, this actual moment you are in. This is where you hold the control.

The practise of Mindfulness and other forms of meditation is beneficial when you are wishing to create inner change.

When you experience any form of trauma as a child, the connections in your brain do not always join up in a healthy way. Mindfulness and meditation practised on a regular basis can bring about calm and clarity and actually reconnect these disjointed physiological links within you.

Mindfulness means focusing on one thing at a time and experiencing just that one thing. You may choose to focus on your breath entering and leaving your body or a candle flame's movement.

Your thoughts will naturally drift away from your focus. Each time you recognise this happening, gently bring yourself back to your focus and continue for a few minutes more.

**Mindfulness exercise:**

Sit comfortably, close your eyes and breathe through your nose. Slowly breathe in and feel the cool air entering your nose. Feel the air at the back of your nose. As you exhale feel the warm air leaving your nostrils. Then, as you breathe, feel the air as it touches the back of your throat. Then feel the air filling your lungs. And finally, feel the air filling your stomach.

Repeat this exercise.

## Meditation

Meditation takes many different forms and my preference is for guided meditations. These are like stories being told to you in which you imagine going on a journey and experiencing the things that you see and hear along the way from the comfort of your chair.

A short guided meditation which you can record at a slow pace on your phone and listen to  whenever you have 15-20 minutes to spare, is as follows:

Make yourself comfortable........ stretch your hands and feet outwards and let them fall into a relaxed, uncrossed position............................close your eyes and take a few deeper breaths............................................................................................ .............................. imagine a rainbow above your head and allow one of those colours to come into your focus.................. let that colour form a small pastel cloud that drops down just above your head........................... as if your head is a magnet to that cloud, allow it to draw down into your mind...................... feel it coming down over your head like a balaclava......... feel it over the back of your head, the sides of your head and over your face............... notice your eyes, closed, relaxed, notice the tiny muscles at the back of your eyes feeling loose and relaxed..........................notice your ears........... your mouth.......... and your jaw................ allow your jaw to relax and drop.............................. picture the colour draining down into your neck and flowing across your shoulders........................... they become heavy and drop......................................... down........................... see the colour flow down your upper arms to your elbows....................................... see the colour flow down your

forearms to your wrists.............. hands and fingers................................. watch the colour radiate out of your finger tips as the tension releases from your body.............................. you may notice a tingling sensation in your finger tips as the tension flows away................................. one hand feels slightly heavier while the other feels slightly warmer................................................................ on the next in breath, breathe the colour into your lungs.......................... see the colour ebb and flow, in and out, as your breathe softly.................................................................................
....... on the next out breath feel your chest relax and become heavy forcing the last of the colour from your lungs....... breathe                                                                         gently
.................................................................................
.................... on the next in breath, breathe the colour into your stomach and see the colour swirling and relaxing..... feel what you feel ..................................... and breathe................................. imagine a hundred coloured butterflies fluttering in your stomach ........................................... and on your next out breath allow the butterflies to settle and stop............................................ breathe gently and on the next out breath allow their wings to close............................................ on the next out breath they fall and disappear leaving a mist of colour that spreads around your sides to your spine............. watch the colour drift up and down your spine............................................. when it is at the top again allow the colour to radiate across your shoulder blades........................... relaxing, softening......................... allow the colour to spread across your middle

back..................... allow the colour to spread across your lower back.................................................... feel the base of your spine and notice the warmth there............ as if there is a heat pad in the back of your chair.......... warming......................... relaxing................................................ see the colour flow through your hips and down your heavy thigh muscles..................... heavy, relaxed.............. let them go........... see the colour flow over your knees............... down your shins.................... down your calf muscles to your ankles............................. your feet............................... and watch the colour flow through he soles of your feet and into the ground................................................ and while the colour flows out, through the soles of your feet, notice that it is still pouring in through the top of your head......... a never ending flow of relaxing energy............................. in through the top of your head........... down through your body........................... out through the soles of your feet...................... in through the top of your head........... down through your body........................... out through the soles of your feet...................... in through the top of your head........... down through your body........................... out through the soles of your feet...................... in through the top of your head........... down through your body........................... out through the soles of your feet...................... in through the top of your head........... down through your body........................... out through the soles of your feet.................................................................................

take a few deeper breathes and open your eyes whenever you feel ready...............................

**Affirmations**

Affirmations are another great way to start having a better relationship with yourself.

Firstly, what negative thoughts do you have about yourself. For instance: "I am unhealthy, I am selfish, I am not good enough, I am unlovable." Now create positive affirmations from these, such as: "I am healthy, I am kind, I am enough, I am loved." Write these affirmations on Post-It notes and stick them anywhere and everywhere – on your phone, the dashboard of your car, on the fridge, on the back of the bathroom door. Anywhere where you regularly look.

Every time you see the affirmation repeat it over and over to yourself while imagining how it feels to be healthy, kind, good enough, and loved. Make that image bright and colourful. You may want to move the messages around to different places every few days so they don't become just part of the furniture that you no longer notice.

Even more powerful than this, is to repeat these affirmations to yourself in front of a mirror, out loud if you can. Notice any resistance to doing this. Acknowledge if it feels fake or silly when you say these things to yourself. Maybe try looking down at your child-self and saying them to him or her first.

Remember, your parents conditioned you to have certain beliefs about yourself and these messages were drip-fed to you daily for years, even if they were said affectionately.

The fact is that you were born as a pretty clear canvas and they imprinted onto you. What you are now telling yourself is no more fake than what they conditioned you to believe because of *their* own conditioning.

## Direction

Most people know what they don't want. When I ask clients: "What do you want? How would you like your life to look? How would you like to feel? What would you like to change?" I am often given a long list of things that they don't want but rarely can they tell me what they do want.

Looking at various aspects of your life you may be able to decide what you like about your life, what you dislike and what you may wish to change.

Rate each item from 0 (extremely discontent) to 5 (highly contented).

| | | | | | | |
|---|---|---|---|---|---|---|
| Mental Health | 0 | 1 | 2 | 3 | 4 | 5 |
| Work | 0 | 1 | 2 | 3 | 4 | 5 |
| Relationships | 0 | 1 | 2 | 3 | 4 | 5 |
| Finances | 0 | 1 | 2 | 3 | 4 | 5 |
| Environment | 0 | 1 | 2 | 3 | 4 | 5 |
| Physical Health | 0 | 1 | 2 | 3 | 4 | 5 |
| Living Skills | 0 | 1 | 2 | 3 | 4 | 5 |
| Social Life | 0 | 1 | 2 | 3 | 4 | 5 |
| Self-Esteem | 0 | 1 | 2 | 3 | 4 | 5 |
| Addictiveness | 0 | 1 | 2 | 3 | 4 | 5 |
| Responsibilities | 0 | 1 | 2 | 3 | 4 | 5 |
| Hope | 0 | 1 | 2 | 3 | 4 | 5 |
| Trust | 0 | 1 | 2 | 3 | 4 | 5 |

You can now see where the lower scores are and ask yourself what would 5 look like. For example, about work: 2 (fairly discontent) What would 5 look like? "Well, I'd be in a different job. I'd earn more money, have less stress, and I'd work outdoors with animals."

Once you know what you do want, you are more likely to find ways of getting there. In the scenario above this might mean retraining, meditating regularly and feeling more deserving of having a better life.

**We get what we FOCUS on**

If you don't want to go to Scotland, and this is what you focus on, you are likely to end up in Scotland. Why? Because when we think about something, whether it is a positive or a negative, we are drawn towards it.

If you try not to think of Father Christmas, it is likely that you are now thinking of and picturing a rather plump, bearded, old man in a red coat and black boots.

If you are driving and looking at an object in the road you don't want to hit, the chances are that you will hit it.

Have you ever bought a new car and then seen that model everywhere? Or, broken-up from a relationship and focused your thoughts on not wanting to be alone - loving couples appear to be prevalent, which reinforces your thinking.

This is why it is so important to focus on the things you do want. Rather than focusing on "I don't want to be alone" start to focus on "I want to be in a loving relationship".

If you do want to go to Scotland, and this is what you focus on, you are more likely to see the route to Scotland become clear to you.

## Your destination

How do you know where you want to go if you have no destination? It would be like getting in the car and just driving around. The journey could be confusing or interesting, and you may end up where you started.

If you got in your car and decided to go to Scotland you would have a destination. Then your thought process would begin to work out how to get you there. As you drive you may see signs for 'The North' and follow them. Maybe you'd plot a route with a map book or programme your sat nav. Whichever method you take, it is likely you'll end up in Scotland.

Life itself can also be this way. Some people like to drift through life without setting themselves any goals or destinations, and that may be okay for them. But how would it be to really live your life on purpose? Actually deciding what you would like from it and getting there?

When you live your life on purpose you are using assertive behaviour. You have decided the way you wish to live your life and know you have every right to live it that way. You are going to be on this planet for such a very short time, especially when you compare it with all the years you have not been on it. You have a right to make the most of it while you are here.

The one thing most people want in this life is to be accepted, and what most people fear is rejection.

In the past it may have seemed easier to do what other people wanted you to do rather than to be assertive and say what you would prefer. You may have been afraid to 'rock the boat' or 'go against the grain' just in case someone thought less of you because they might feel some emotional discomfort and blame you. You needed to feel liked to avoid your fears of rejection.

Now you realise that you were allowing dominating people to take advantage of you and you were encouraging their selfish behaviour. You now see that these dominating people were afraid of being rejected. They needed to feel in control to avoid their fears of rejection.

You can easily get your needs met without violating the rights of others and that is why you have decided to stand up for yourself from this day forward. You recognise that by respecting yourself you are training others to respect you and by showing them respect you are treating them as you demand to be treated. You expect respect and respect others in return.

As a child you may have been conditioned to believe you had to put others before yourself and to  put their needs above your own. You are not responsible for protecting other people's feelings, especially if it is to the detriment of your own feelings.

You can now see that by taking responsibility for other people's feelings you were effectively telling them that you knew what was best for them and that they were not as capable as you. Now you realise that you are equal to others and you respect them as much as you respect yourself.

You have every right to express your emotions and to feel emotional because all your emotions are valid. You can now see that you are equal to others and have as much right as anyone else to be treated fairly and with respect.

You now recognise that you can easily say "no" without feeling any of those old uncomfortable feelings. You have every right to go where you want; say what you want and be who you want to be without fearing what others may think or say about you.

You  are your own judge and  you are at peace with your decisions and your behaviours.

From now on you will refuse to suffer in silence or say "it's fine" when it is not.

In the past you may have felt uncomfortable asking for your own needs to be met and you went along with what others wanted to do in fear of getting it wrong and feeling humiliated. Now you can see that your choices and decisions are as valid and worthy as anyone else's.

Behaving assertively now comes naturally to you.

Every day you notice yourself thinking more positively; experiencing more positive feelings and behaving in a calm and assertive way.

If you don't want to do something you simply say "no". If you wish to be on your own or do something by yourself you know you have every right to do so.

You have every right to do things the way you wish to without having to explain your self  to others or make excuses for your behaviour.

You find that more and more you are becoming more honest, because what you say is not intended to upset or hurt anyone. It is logical and factual and relevant.

You have a right to ask questions and challenge traditions; to ask for help if you need assistance and you have every right to learn by making mistakes.

You feel empowered to act now, and you know no one has a right to place you in uncomfortable situations.

You find yourself expecting to be respected and you respect those around you.

You find yourself spending more time with people who love and support you and you have every right to spend less time with anybody who puts you down or repeatedly criticises you. Every day you become interested to find your are speaking up for yourself and realising how easy it is and how good it feels to have your voice heard and respected.

You are equal to all other humans and as such have a right to share your thoughts and feelings with others as they too enjoy sharing their thoughts and feelings with you. Now you can see that you deserve to be appreciated as you refuse to be taken for granted.

You are already more assertive and confident and this is why people are now treating you with more respect. Every day you are becoming more assertive and your belief in yourself and your own abilities grows stronger. Every day you tell yourself "I am capable. I am deserving" and you find life is calmer and you feel happier.

As children we were conditioned with rules of how to behave and what to do and what not to do and this created submissive children and then passive adults. You no longer have to follow those rules because you are not a child any more and you can make your own rules.

You have a right to put your own needs first especially if other people are taking advantage of you. And now you can see that those old feelings that stopped you from being assertive, confident and respected were given to you by people who were afraid of losing control.

Create this scene in your mind, if you will. You are sitting in your own private cinema on a soft, velvet seat. Feel yourself sinking deeper down into those soft cushions.

Looks at the screen as the film starts to play and watch how an assertive person on the screen moves and behaves. They are neither passive and shy or aggressive and bullying. They simply operate for themselves. They are their own judge.

Watch this person stand up for what they believe is right and fair, listen to how they speak, notice their body language, and see them respected for their views.

When you are ready imagine yourself stepping into that person on the screen and experience what it is like to be confident and positive and able to assert your own needs. See yourself doing things the way they do and speaking in an assertive manner.

Now close your eyes and replay that film. Really experience what it is like to think, feel and behave assertively …....................

You are now becoming a much more assertive person and you speak up for yourself and never allow yourself to be treated how you feel you were previously treated.

Place this new you into a future situation where you need to assert yourself; perhaps this is a similar scenario to ones you've experienced in the past and weren't happy with. Hear what you say; your voice is steady and clear and you find it easy to speak up for yourself.

Notice how you now command respect  and hear how effectively you communicate with others and experience good feelings inside you as you describe the changes you'd like making or putting your ideas or opinions forward.

Close your eyes again, replay that film and  really experience how you think, feel and behave in this scenario …....................

Be specific about what you do and don't want and what you would like to happen, ensuring that the requested changes are reasonable and considering other people's needs too.

Every day you are feeling more and more confident. You are thinking more and more positively and you notice how easy it is to behave assertively.

You notice that you give people genuine compliments and now accept compliments by just saying "thank you" without embellishing further.

You are not a child any more and as an adult you have a right to do and say what you feel is right. By asserting yourself in this way you are showing others that you expect respect.

You notice how much more relaxed you feel. You respond slowly, calmly and assertively to all situations.

You have walked the same path for many years. This path was created for you and you have blindly followed its track every day. Now you have forged a new path of your own creation and every day that you walk this path it becomes stronger, clearer and more defined.

One day soon, the old path will lose its definition and faded away.

Every day you feel happier and freer to live the life you wish to live.

You believe in yourself, you know you are capable and deserving of happiness, and the respect you have for yourself will cause the Ripple Effect which ensures that others treat you with the respect you deserve also.

## Beliefs

We all have beliefs and mainly they were cultivated in childhood. Your beliefs developed because you were verbally told, metaphorically told and suggested to, and your experiences were interpreted in certain ways by you through your filter.

You took on board this information and reinforced it with your thoughts and feelings until it became your belief system.

A belief can be a very powerful tool, and just like the Cycle for Success, what you believe can also result in your happiness.

A belief is the meaning you put on something through your thoughts. You can choose to continue with a particular train of thought or you can create a new positive meaning and develop a new belief.

For instance, I was arranging a client's next appointment and said it would be on the thirteenth of the month.

His face dropped and he said: "The thirteenth? That's not going to be a good day." He went on to explain that his dog died on November 13 when he was 10-years-old and since then the thirteenth has been a bad day for him. He added that it wasn't just the date that he believed would be bad but anything regarding the number 13 was to be avoided.

He had formed the belief (or the thoughts and feelings) that bad things happen around the number 13. So, when he wakes up on the thirteenth of any month, he thinks: "Today is gong to be a bad day," and he starts to feel demoralised or worried. He is absorbed into the Cycle of Doom.

For me, the number 13 is one of my favourite numbers, I have lots of favourite numbers. 3, 6, 13 and 21 are my most favourite. I believe that any of these numbers are particularly lucky for me and so you can imagine how my thoughts, feelings, behaviours and results reflect from this belief.

I also believe I was born lucky; I don't want much, but I always get what I do want; bizarre things happen to me, and I have a terrible sense of direction.

These beliefs probably stem from my childhood messages and experiences, but I actively encourage any belief that is going to benefit me and actively discourage any belief that does not serve me well.

Mainly these beliefs serve me well, although it does mean at times people find it difficult to believe some of the things that happen to me and I do have a tendency to get lost.

This thinking or believing, is the same way that lucky charms work. Who hasn't got a pair of lucky pants? If you are given an item, say a pebble, and you are told it is a lucky pebble, you can choose to believe it has special powers if you want to.

If you are carrying that pebble when something good happens, you may think to yourself: "It was probably because I had my lucky pebble in my pocket." This thought will reinforce your belief.

If something bad happens, you will probably not associate it with your pebble because your belief is that it is a lucky pebble and not an unlucky pebble (the Velcro Effect comes into play and the idea sticks rather than slides away).

This belief can grow and develop and become so strong that whenever you have the pebble with you, you actually believe you will have a good day, and because you believe and think this (the Cycle for Success is activated by your positive thinking) the chances are that you will indeed have a good day. This will, once again, reinforce your belief.

Of course this line of thinking and believing could also be detrimental to your feelings, for example if you lost the pebble or forgot to take it with you.

If, however, someone gives you a lucky pebble and you choose to think: "What a load of old rot," regardless of whether anything good or bad happens to you, you are not going to relate it to the pebble and therefore it has no significance (the Teflon Effect enables the idea to slide away).

It is important to realise that it is the belief (your thinking) that holds the power and not the pebble. My guess is that prayers, spells and rituals manifest by the same principle. What you believe will happen, will happen. Believing, and I mean truly believing, is a very powerful tool.

Focus boards (also known as vision boards) work in the same way. You simply decide what you do want and place it on your focus board. You can cut out pictures from magazines or write words or draw pictures. The more imaginative the better. Look at this board every day and imagine how it will feel when it actually happens. Visualise how you look, think, feel and behave when what you want materialises.

I decided to try out Cosmic Ordering a few years ago, after several household bills and red reminders arrived through my letterbox. I looked up at whatever or whoever might be listening and said: "Please could I have some cheques through my door instead?"

The next day, to my great amusement, a blank chequebook arrived.

I looked up again and said: "Thank you. Very funny. Please could I have some hard cash through my door?"

I hadn't really taken it very seriously, and soon forgot about my request.

Later that week I helped a friend pick up wet walnuts and windfall apples and was given a basket full to take home.

As there were far too many for me to eat, I bagged them up and put them by my front gate. Within hours pound coins were dropping onto my doormat in exchange for the produce.

## Visualisation

Whatever you want, whether that is to be a milkman, write a book, travel to Africa, fly in a hot air balloon, or to create health, wealth or happiness, you can make it happen. Form a strong visual image in your mind of what that will look like for you. Make this image as colourful, meaningful and three dimensional as possible and really feel what it feels like to be there already.

When you focus directly and intensely on what you would like to achieve, it is much more likely that it will become a reality for you.

Sometimes, when you get what you want it can appear to be detrimental elsewhere. Say you wanted £100,000 and when this manifested it was because your relationship had ended and you had to sell your house.

# Be careful what you wish for, you might just get it.

# WORK SHEETS

## Challenging Negative Thoughts Week One

Notice Negative Thinking and write it down

e.g. "This food is just going to be awful. I'm a terrible cook. No one will eat it and they'll think I'm stupid."

## Challenging Negative Thoughts Week Two

| Situation | Negative Thought | Feeling |
| --- | --- | --- |
| e.g. In the kitchen | I'm a rubbish cook | Hopeless<br>Sad |

**Challenging Negative Thoughts Week Three**

| Situation | Negative Thought | Feeling | Whereabouts |
|---|---|---|---|
| e.g. In the kitchen | I'm a rubbish cook | Hopeless | Chest |

**Challenging Negative Thoughts Week Four**

| Negative Thought | Feeling | Whereabouts | Behaviour |
| --- | --- | --- | --- |
| I'm a rubbish cook | Hopeless | Chest, heavy | Cried and put dinner in bin |

## Challenging Negative Thoughts Week Five

| Negative Thought | Feeling | Whereabouts | Behaviour | Result |
| --- | --- | --- | --- | --- |
| I'm a rubbish cook | Hopeless | Chest, heavy | Dinner in bin | Hungry |

## Challenging Negative Thoughts Week Six

| Negative Thought % | Feeling % | Challenge Thought | Feeling % |
|---|---|---|---|
| I'm rubbish cook 95% | Sad 100% | Made nice meal before | Sad? 5% |

## Challenging Negative Thoughts Week Seven

| Negative Thought % | Feeling % | Behaviour | Result |
| --- | --- | --- | --- |
| I'm a rubbish cook 95% | Sad 100% | Cried, dinner in bin | Hungry |

**Challenging Negative Thoughts Week Seven Continued ..........**

| Challenge Thought | Feeling % | Behaviour | Result |
|---|---|---|---|
| Made nice meal before | Sad 5% | Found recipe | Happy and full |

## Mind Reading and Fortune Telling

| Forthcoming situation | Prediction | Reality (fill in after event) |
|---|---|---|
| e.g. Cooking for friends | It'll be a disaster | Evening was great fun |

| What I think someone thought about me | More realistic thought (or ask them) |
|---|---|
| e.g. She's a rubbish cook and friend | They like me, for me |

# SUMMING UP

How you were when you picked up this book was the sum total of everything you had experienced in life up to that point. Your perception of all these experiences was determined by how you interpreted the first two years of your life – whether you felt secure or insecure.

If you felt secure you would likely have grown into an assertive, Adult person with healthy high self-esteem and it is unlikely that this book is particularly relevant to you.

However, if you felt insecure and grew into a passive, aggressive or passive-aggressive person who spent much of their time in the Parent and Child roles, you may have had lower self-esteem and this guide may have been a game-changer for you.

You have now read where your thoughts, feelings and behaviours originated from and how you have repeated and practised them until they became habits you feared to change.

By practising assertive behaviour and an Adult stance your self-esteem is developing and growing, and with healthy self-esteem comes feelings of security.

By practising positive thinking, meditation and visualising what you do want, your life is becoming everything you've ever dreamt it could be.

# GLOSSARY

ACCEPTANCE – feeling at ease about a situation that cannot be changed.

ADULT – an adult is a grown-up person. A person in Adult is factual, logical and rational.

AFFIRMATIONS – words or phrases repeated to the self to undermine negative beliefs.

ASSERTIVENESS – behaviours which reflect a person's respect for their self and others.

ATTATCHMENT STYLES – how people form relationships based on their mother/child bonding.

AUTOPILOT – using subconscious behaviours without conscious thought.

AVOIDANT – subconsciously pushing people away or avoiding uncomfortable emotions.

BELIEFS – thoughts based on messages people learned were true regardless of whether they were.

BLUEPRINT – Expectations of the self and the world, developed in early life.

BRICKWORK – thoughts, feelings and behaviours repeated in a predetermined pattern.

CHANGE – consciously choosing and practising different ways of thinking, feeling and behaving.

CHILD – a child is a person under the age of 16. A person in Child is replaying childhood feelings.

194

COGNITIVE BEHAVIOURIAL THERAPY – learning how thoughts impact feelings/behaviours.

CONDITIONING – how people learn to behave by being punished or praised or by copying.

CONSCIOUS – knowingly behaving in various ways.

CONTOL – a person feeling that they have some power over a situation.

CONTROLLING – a behaviour which causes another person to behave as someone wishes them to.

DISOCIATE – becoming emotionally disengaged from reality.

DOMINO EFFECT – the knock-on effect from one generation to the next.

DRAMA TRIANGLE – when people behave in ways that cause emotional discomfort.

EXTERNAL WORLD – anything outside a person's psyche such as people, objects, events etc.

FALSE BELIEFS - thoughts based on untrue messages people learned were true.

FEAR – uncomfortable emotions which prevent a person from making changes.

FORTUNE TELLING – predicting the experience of up-coming events or situations.

FOUNDATION – a person's parents and how they influenced who they are.

FRAMEWORK – the conditioning people learn from their parents' behaviours.

GROUNDWORK – the effects on a person passed down  from the generations before them.

HABITS – repeating behaviours until they become automatic.

HYPER-VIGILANT – being super observant, usually to avoid or control difficult situations.

INNER VOICE/DIALOGUE – a person's self-talk within their own heads.

INTERNAL WORLD – how a person thinks and feels about themselves and the world around them.
MAGICAL THINKING – irrationally believing that certain behaviours will control outcomes.

MEDITATION – focusing on calming environments, objects or sounds to quieten the mind.

MESSAGES – parents' actions, gestures, behaviours, voice tone and words a child  experiences.

METAPHORICAL MIRROR – an imaginary mirror that reflects a parent's view of a child.

MINDFULLNESS – the ability to think, feel and behave in the now, not in the past or the future.

MIND-READING – predicting or guessing what people are thinking.

NEGATIVE THINKING (OVER-USE OF) – compulsively thinking that bad things will happen.

OBJECTIFYING – feeling that an object provides the security of being with mother.

OBSESSIVE COMPULSIVE DISORDER – repeating sets of behaviours in order to feel okay.

PARENT – a mother or father. A person in Parent is copying their parents' words and behaviours.

PEOPLE PLEASER – a person who tries to manipulate others by their perceived helpful behaviour.

RE-PARENTING – treating yourself as an assertive parent with healthy self-esteem would have.

REPEAT CYCLES – subconsciously using habits to recreate similar patterns throughout life.

RIPPLE EFFECT – how a person's behaviours impact on people and situations around them.

FAMILY RULES – a person's ways of thinking, feeling and behaving acceptable to their family.

SCAFFOLDING – avoidant and controlling methods used to cope with uncomfortable emotions.

SELF-ESTEEM – how a person feels about their self and the respect they show their self.

SMART BRAIN – the automatic, subconscious way people understand themselves and others.

SNAGGING – habits and fears that prevent a person self-improving.

SUBCONSCIOUS/UNCONSCIOUS – automatic thoughts and behaviours.

TOWER – the combined Groundwork, Foundation, Framework, Brickwork, Wiring and Windows.

TRIGGERS – sounds, sights, tastes, smells, or feelings that evoke certain memories or behaviours.

UNDERMINERS – internal and external messages that try to sabotage a person's self-improvement.

UNDERPINNING – growing healthy self-esteem to counteract negative childhood messages.

VELCRO AN TEFLON EFFECTS – keeping or letting go of messages that do or do not 'fit'.

VISUALISATION – thinking about positive life changes and feeling how this would feel in reality.

WINDOWS (FILTER) – a person's perspective of themselves and others.

WIRING (SMART BRAIN) – a person's understanding based on learned behaviours/conditioning.

Printed in Poland
by Amazon Fulfillment
Poland Sp. z o.o., Wrocław

63385244R00112